First World War
and Army of Occupation
War Diary
France, Belgium and Germany

36 DIVISION
Divisional Troops
153 Brigade Royal Field Artillery
21 January 1916 - 31 December 1918

WO95/2496/3

The Naval & Military Press Ltd
www.nmarchive.com
Published in association with The National Archives

Published by

The Naval & Military Press Ltd

Unit 10 Ridgewood Industrial Park,

Uckfield, East Sussex,

TN22 5QE England

Tel: +44 (0) 1825 749494

www.naval-military-press.com

www.nmarchive.com

This diary has been reprinted in facsimile from the original. Any imperfections are inevitably reproduced and the quality may fall short of modern type and cartographic standards.

© Crown Copyright
Images reproduced by permission of The National Archives, London, England, 2015.

Contents

Document type	Place/Title	Date From	Date To
Heading	WO95/2496/3		
Heading	36th Division. 153rd Brigade R.F.A. 1915 Nov-Feb 1919		
Heading	153rd Bde. R.F.A. Vol. I. Jan 16. Feb 19		
Miscellaneous			
War Diary	Lancheres.	21/01/1916	21/01/1916
War Diary	Watiehurt	21/01/1916	21/01/1916
War Diary	Hurt.	21/01/1916	21/01/1916
War Diary	Brutelles.	24/01/1916	24/01/1916
War Diary	Sallenelles.	24/01/1916	31/01/1916
War Diary	Lancheres & District.	01/02/1916	29/02/1916
War Diary	Martinsart.	01/04/1916	12/04/1916
War Diary	Pernois.	29/02/1916	06/03/1916
War Diary	Martinsart.	06/03/1916	31/03/1916
War Diary	Martinsart.	28/03/1916	07/05/1916
Heading	153rd Bde. R.F.A. Vols: 2, 3		
War Diary	Martinsart.	08/05/1916	31/05/1916
Heading	36th Divisional Artillery. 153rd. Brigade. Royal Field Artillery. June 1916		
War Diary	Martinsart.	01/06/1916	23/06/1916
War Diary	Mesnil.	24/06/1916	30/06/1916
Heading	36th Divisional Artillery. 153rd Brigade. Royal Field Artillery. July 1916		
Heading	153rd Brigade R.F.A.		
War Diary	Mesnil.	01/07/1916	12/07/1916
War Diary	Hedauville Forceville.	13/07/1916	22/07/1916
War Diary	Neuve Eglise.	23/07/1916	31/07/1916
War Diary	T.21.d.2.1	01/08/1916	31/08/1916
War Diary	Map 1/20,000. 28. S.W. 4 Ploegsteert	01/09/1916	02/09/1916
War Diary	T.21.d.2.1	03/09/1916	13/09/1916
War Diary	T.15.d.1020	14/09/1916	30/09/1916
War Diary	Map Reference 1-20,000 28.S.W. 4. Ploegsteert T.21.d.2.1	01/10/1916	31/10/1916
War Diary	Map 1-20,000 28. S.W. Ploegsteert T.21.d.20.10	01/11/1916	31/03/1917
War Diary	Lumbres.	01/04/1917	30/04/1917
War Diary	Dranoutre M.35.d.40.20	01/05/1917	30/06/1917
War Diary	Metz-En Couture.	01/10/1917	20/11/1917
War Diary	Hermies	21/11/1917	21/11/1917
War Diary	SE Of Demicourt J.18	23/11/1917	25/11/1917
War Diary	SE. Of Demicourt K 15b.	26/11/1917	29/11/1917
War Diary	S.W. Of Lock 4. K.15.a.	30/11/1917	30/11/1917
War Diary	Ref. Sheet 57 C N.E. K.14.b.9.4	01/12/1917	05/12/1917
War Diary	J.30.c.0.0	06/12/1917	06/12/1917
War Diary	Sheet 57 c. N.E. J.30.c.0.0	07/12/1917	12/12/1917
War Diary	Sheet 57c. N.E. K.30.c.d.	12/12/1917	14/12/1917
War Diary	K.30.d.2.0	15/12/1917	19/12/1917
War Diary	Q.12.a.25.60	20/12/1917	26/12/1917
War Diary	Le Translor	27/12/1917	01/01/1918
War Diary	Ville-Sur-Corbie	02/01/1918	02/01/1918
War Diary	Hamel.	03/01/1918	07/01/1918

War Diary	Hangest.	08/01/1918	10/01/1918
War Diary	Roye.	11/01/1918	12/01/1918
War Diary	Sheet 66.a.	13/01/1918	13/01/1918
War Diary	F.22.d.83	14/01/1918	27/01/1918
War Diary	F.22.d.8.3	22/01/1918	31/01/1918
War Diary	Sheet 62 B S.W. F.23.d.8.5	01/02/1918	20/02/1918
War Diary	Offoy.	21/02/1918	28/02/1918
Heading	36th Divisional Artillery. 153rd Brigade R.F.A. March 1918		
War Diary	Gd Seraucourt.	01/03/1918	23/03/1918
War Diary	Bacquencourt. I.35	23/03/1918	23/03/1918
War Diary	Flavy-Le-Meldeux V5	24/03/1918	24/03/1918
War Diary	Freniches.	24/03/1918	25/03/1918
War Diary	Beaulieu.	25/03/1918	25/03/1918
War Diary	Avricourt.	25/03/1918	25/03/1918
War Diary	Balny Farm.	26/03/1918	26/03/1918
War Diary	Gury La Cense Farm.	26/03/1918	26/03/1918
War Diary	St. Claud Farm.	27/03/1918	30/03/1918
War Diary	Grand Fresnoy.	31/03/1918	31/03/1918
Heading	36th Divisional Artillery. 153rd Brigade R.F.A. April 1918		
War Diary	Wariville & Lortiet.	01/04/1918	01/04/1918
War Diary	Francastel.	02/04/1918	02/04/1918
War Diary	Morvillers St. Saturnin.	03/04/1918	07/04/1918
War Diary	Moyencourt Sous Poix.	08/04/1918	10/04/1918
War Diary	Renancourt Par Amiens.	11/04/1918	13/04/1918
War Diary	Amiens.	14/04/1918	14/04/1918
War Diary	Poperinghe.	15/04/1918	15/04/1918
War Diary	Berthen.	16/04/1918	22/04/1918
War Diary	Hamhoek.	23/04/1918	25/04/1918
War Diary	Ypres.	26/04/1918	31/05/1918
War Diary	In the Field.	01/06/1918	05/06/1918
War Diary	Field.	05/06/1918	30/06/1918
War Diary	Handekot.	01/07/1918	04/07/1918
War Diary	Hardifort.	05/07/1918	05/07/1918
War Diary	Berthen.	06/07/1918	31/08/1918
Heading	36th Division Artillery.	06/10/1918	06/10/1918
War Diary	Neuve Eglise.	01/09/1918	18/09/1918
War Diary	Croix De Poperinghe.	19/09/1918	20/09/1918
War Diary	Haandekot.	21/09/1918	26/09/1918
War Diary	A.28.d.	27/09/1918	27/09/1918
War Diary	Ramparts.	28/09/1918	28/09/1918
War Diary	D.25.c. Control.	29/09/1918	30/09/1918
War Diary	K.140.b.57	30/09/1918	31/10/1918
War Diary	Lauwe	01/11/1918	30/11/1918
War Diary	Tourcoing.	01/12/1918	31/12/1918

WO 2496/3
95

36TH DIVISION

153RD BRIGADE R.F.A.

1915 Nov JAN 1916-FEB 1919

153rd Bde: R.Ha.
Vol I

Nov.

Jan '16
Feb '19

36

Army Form C. 2118

WAR DIARY
or
INTELLIGENCE SUMMARY
(Erase heading not required.)

153rd Brigade. Royal Field Artillery.

Place	Date	Hour	Summary of Events and Information	Remarks and references to Appendices
			The Brigade left BORDON by rail on the 26th Nov 1915, embarked at SOUTHAMPTON the same evening, reached HAVRE next morning. Entrained at HAVRE on the evening of the 27th Nov. detrained at PONT RÉMY and marched to Billets at LONG and LONGUET on the 28th Nov. The strength of this Brigade and list of Officers on embarkation was as follows :— Lt.Col. V. Paget. R.F.A. Commanding. Lieut. P.J. Flanagan. Adjutant. 2/Lieut. R.E.N. Braden. Orderly Officer. Captains :— W.A. Nicholls. W. McC. Cowan. C.A.L. Brownlow. A.H. Smith. A.H. Wood. Lieutenants :— H.J. Wellingham. W.E. Loudoun-Shand. J.C. Dunkley. V.R. Krohn. 2/Lieuts :— J.C. Dunkley. R.W. Urwin. J.J. Gaynor. J. Cashin. G. Huskisson. R. Powell. F.I. Cotching. W. Montserrat. M. Cane. D.R. Cartwright. C. Williamson. R.H. Browne. Attached: Lt. J. Paul. A.V.C. Lt. J. Gavin. R.A.M.C. N.C.Os & Men. 734.	

Army Form C. 2118

WAR DIARY
or
INTELLIGENCE SUMMARY
(Erase heading not required.)

153rd Brigade. Royal Field Artillery.

Place	Date	Hour	Summary of Events and Information	Remarks and references to Appendices
			The Brigade proceeded from LONG by MARCH ROUTE on the 23rd of January 1916, and billetted as follows :—	
			Headquarters — LANCHERES.	
			"A" Battery — WATHIEHURT.	
			"B" Battery — HURT.	
			"C" Battery — BRUTELLES.	
			"D" Battery — BRUTELLES.	
			Ammunition Column — SALLENELLES.	

K Pouget
Lieut Col RFA
Commandant 153 Bde RFA

Army Form C. 2118.

WAR DIARY
or
INTELLIGENCE SUMMARY.

(Erase heading not required.)

153 Bde R.F.A.

Instructions regarding War Diaries and Intelligence Summaries are contained in F. S. Regs., Part II. and the Staff Manual respectively. Title pages will be prepared in manuscript.

Place	Date	Hour	Summary of Events and Information	Remarks and references to Appendices
Lavellois	21.1.16		Brigade Headquarters arrived from Longe	
Fatihurst	21.1.16		A Battery arrived from Longe	
Hurst	21.1.16		B Battery arrived from Longe	
Boutillio	21.1.16		C Battery arrived from Longe	
Boutillio	21.1.16		D Battery arrived from Longe	
Lavellois	21.1.16		Ammunition Column arrived from Longe	
	21.1.16 to 31.1.16		All Batteries & Column underwent training during the time the Brigade was in this area.	

W.H.A. Liddle
Capt. R.F.A.
Comdg 153 Bde R.F.A.

153 Bde R.F.A.

Army Form C. 2118.

WAR DIARY
or
INTELLIGENCE SUMMARY.
(Erase heading not required.)

Instructions regarding War Diaries and Intelligence Summaries are contained in F. S. Regs., Part II. and the Staff Manual respectively. Title pages will be prepared in manuscript.

Place	Date	Hour	Summary of Events and Information	Remarks and references to Appendices
Lanchères & District	1/2/16 to 2/2/16		Batteries Column underwent training during this period	
	2/2/16 to 10/2/16			
	20/2/16		Firing Practice carried out by Batteries	
	27/2/16		Brigade moved to PONT REMY. Batteries & Column moved independently. Bad weather caused delay en route.	
	29/2/16		Brigade moved to TERNOIS.	

W.B. Nicholls Capt R.F.A.
Comdg 153 Bde R.F.A.

WAR DIARY or INTELLIGENCE SUMMARY

Army Form C. 2118.
vol 4
153 RFA
XXXVI

Place	Date	Hour	Summary of Events and Information	Remarks and references to Appendices
Mailly-Maillet	1-2nd		Normal trench warfare. 6 R.D. Batteries registered R.25.b.10.	
	2-3rd		6 R.D. Batteries again registered. "B" Battery out line. Hostile fire fairly quiet. A dummy gun appears to have been placed behind hedge surrounding cemetery at R.19.d.70.53.d. Our fire in BEAUCOURT STATION & Railway sidings apparently good-heavy. In the afternoon	
		10 pm to 10.30 pm	20 – 5.9 fell in MESNIL.	
	3 to 4th		Comparatively quiet. A few 150 9m were fired into MESNIL & its vicinity, was shelled by 77mm probably aiming at working parties along the Railway. A few French mortars were fired into Nahout area.	
	4-5th		Hostile artillery fire normal.	
	5-6th		Normal trench warfare.	
	6-7th		Quiet all day. At 9.pm the enemy started a fairly heavy bombardment behind HAMEL & vicinity & shelled MESNIL heavily (between 200 & 300 shells – a good many 150 mm H.E. fell into this area) also the position of B & C Batteries were shelled with 77mm guns. Our front was also shelled by 77mm field guns. Our guns retaliated at once at a fairly rapid rate of fire and HAMEL sector & at a very slow rate of fire on the THIEPVAL Wood sub-sector. As bombardment was heaviest in the North section on our front line, A/153 was turned on to reinforce our extreme left in Q.17.d. Everything quiet after 10 pm. No increase in enemies infantry appear to have taken place. As far as can be judged.	
	7-8th		Nothing of importance happened.	
	8-9th 4.pm.		About 4.pm 30 rounds of 150 mm H.E. fell into Q.9.C.2.9 otherwise quiet all day.	
	9-10th		Several trains seen moving from BAPAUME to ACHIET-LEGRAND & from PUISIEUX to IRLES, at slow speed. Artillery fire normal.	
	10-11		Wire cutting practice. Instruction of junior officers.	
	11-12		Do	

15 Bde RFA

Army Form C. 2118.

WAR DIARY
or
INTELLIGENCE SUMMARY.
(Erase heading not required.)

Instructions regarding War Diaries and Intelligence Summaries are contained in F. S. Regs., Part II. and the Staff Manual respectively. Title pages will be prepared in manuscript.

Place	Date	Hour	Summary of Events and Information	Remarks and references to Appendices
Demuin	29.2.16 to 6.3.16		The Brigade remained at Demuin for this period.	
	6.3.16		Brigade moved to Acheux. Gun Positions had been arranged for by advance parties & Batteries moved up to Positions in the line	
Martinsart	6.3.16		C Battery came into action, taking over Position from 3rd N.R.Bde.	
	7.3.16		Right Section B Battery occupies Position at Mesnil	
			Right Section D Battery occupies Position at Martinsart	
			Left Section D Battery occupies Position at Auchonvillers	
			Right Section A Battery occupies Position at Mesnil	
	8.3.16		Batteries registered Zones	
	8.3.16 to 12.3.16			
	10/11/12 3.16		Hostile Bombardment on Mesnil – Martinsart. Wire cutting carried out by Batteries. Normal trench warfare	
	12.3.16 to 31.3.16		Gun Pits & Dug outs were commenced & continued during this period. Normal trench warfare.	
	28.3.16		Left Section D Battery completed new Position at Martinsart	

W.B. Webb Lt Col
Comdg 15th Bde RFA 14th April 16

Army Form C. 2118.

WAR DIARY
or
INTELLIGENCE SUMMARY.
(Erase heading not required.)

April 1916

Instructions regarding War Diaries and Intelligence Summaries are contained in F. S. Regs., Part II. and the Staff Manual respectively. Title pages will be prepared in manuscript.

Place	Date	Hour	Summary of Events and Information	Remarks and references to Appendices
Martinsart	12-13		Wire cutting practice. Instruction of Junior Officers.	
	13.14		Hostile Artillery quiet. During hour ending 14.5.16. a considerable enemy air service appears to be kept up by the enemy. Liones of 5 + 6 aircraft running all hours of its day. Wire cutting practice + Registration. THIEPVAL Wood shelled by 77mm fairly heavily.	
	14.15			
	15.16		Hostile Artillery active on Q.30.c + Q.36.a during the day. New trench observed being dug at R.16.a probably leading to O.P. Numerous men seen travelling from BIHUCOURT to ACHIET-LE-GRAND + ACHIET-LE-GRAND to BAPAUME. MESNIL RIDGE shelled with 20-77mm. 2 Observation Balloons overhead on bearings 43° + 69°. Numerous taken from Q.22.d.95. Normal Trench Warfare.	
	16-17			
	17-18			
	18.19		HAMEL – AUCHONVILLERS shelled by 77mm on several occasions during day. Our service did usual daily registration, wire cutting + retaliation when asked for by Infantry.	
	19.20		29-77mm landed in MESNIL + MESNIL Ridge in the morning.	
	20-21		Quiet all day.	
	21.22		Fairly quiet all day. In the night of 22-23rd a Bombardment was opened by us between 9-20 + 11-25 on the THIEPVAL Sector, to which the enemy replied by a heavy barrage on the front line trenches. Trench Mortars were located in THIEPVAL CHATEAU R.25.c. + subjects to shrapnel + H.E. fire.	
	22-23		Quiet normal	
	23-24		Do Do	
	24-25		Observation Balloon seen greater part of day at bearing 95° 30' taken from Q.28.d.85.88. Hostile Artillery fire quiet.	

Army Form C. 2118

WAR DIARY
or
INTELLIGENCE SUMMARY
(Erase heading not required.)

April 1916.

Place	Date	Hour	Summary of Events and Information	Remarks and references to Appendices
Martinsart	25-26		Trench Mortars fairly active. A good deal of transport seen on PUISIEUX - ACHIET Road. Enemy aircraft over our lines - fired on by A.A. guns.	
	26-27		Normal.	
	27-28		A F.O. Post observed at R.25.c.30.60, + what is apparently, a German O.P. was observed from Q.35.a.28.78. - magnetic bearing from 42°. A searchlight was observed, the ray of which came from THIEPVAL.	
	28-29		MESNIL shelled heavily during the day. A great deal of mechanical + horse drawn transport seen on road towards PUISIEUX. 3 search lights seen from direction of LA BOISELLE.	
	29-30		113 * 105 mm fell all round Q.27.d. with all indications that Registration was being carried out by aeroplane on "A" Battery's gun position.	

R.C. Thorn
Lieut-Colonel. R.F.A.
Commanding 153. Bde. R.F.A.

Army Form C. 2118.

WAR DIARY
or
INTELLIGENCE SUMMARY
(Erase heading not required.)

MAY 1916.   153rd Brigade R.F.A.

Place	Date	Hour	Summary of Events and Information	Remarks and references to Appendices
MARTINSART.	1st May 1916		Enemy activity normal.	
	2nd		Quiet all day	
	3rd		Throughout the day hostile artillery active. Many 77 m/m were fired into Q24d & Q 30 d. We retaliated.	
	4th		French Mortars active. THIEPVAL Sector (R.25.a & Q 30d being subjected to considerable bombardment.	
	5th		Early in the morning two bombs were dropped by hostile aeroplane on horse lines in MARTINSART. During the day 12 77.m.m fell into MARTINSART. On the night 5th/6th for about an hour we bombarded the enemy trenches in conjunction with the 32nd Division.	
	6th		Quiet. A few 77 m.m. sent over into MARTINSART in the afternoon. Hostile plane dropped a bomb on Q 33 b. doing no harm.	
	7th		Nothing of importance happened during the day. On the night 7/8th the infantry carried out a raid on the enemy trenches. After 3/4 of an hour bombardment the infantry were enabled, owing to the wire cutting done by B/153 to reach the enemy's lines without difficulty & return to their own lines with very few casualties. No prisoners were taken. The wire done by B/153 in this raid was mentioned in

XXXVI

153rd Bde:
R.F.A.
vols: 2, 3

Army Form C. 2118.

May 1916.   2.

WAR DIARY
or
INTELLIGENCE SUMMARY
(Erase heading not required.)

153rd Brigade R.F.A.

Place	Date	Hour	Summary of Events and Information	Remarks and references to Appendices
MARTINSART.	8th May 1916		in the General Officer Commanding in Chief's dispatch.	
	9th		Aircraft active on both sides. Throughout the day a large number of 77m/m were fired into Q 27 d. Q 28 r Q 34.	
	10th		Nothing happened today worth recording.	
	11th		Quiet all day. Q 29 b was shelled by a few 77 m/m	
	12th		Shrapnel normal.	
	13th		Hostile artillery fire fairly active on Q 33.	
	14th		Quiet.	
	15th		Normal trench warfare.	
	16th		Several 77 mm fired into Q23 b. during the day, otherwise very little firing. Trench mortars active on Q 23 d r Q 17 c. r d. Hostile artillery active between midnight r 2.30 am firing into same area.	
	17th		Quiet all day.	
	18th		A few shells put into THIEPVAL Wood.	
	19th		Hostile artillery fairly active all day.	
	20th		Q 33 shelled by 150 mm, remainder of fire during the day consisted of 77 mm (fairly numerous)	
	21st		Hostile artillery again very active. Q 28 r Q 33 receiving nearly all the enemy's attention. Their A.A. guns were also active against our aeroplanes. The	

WAR DIARY or INTELLIGENCE SUMMARY

Army Form C. 2118.

May 1916

153rd Brigade R.F.A.

Place	Date	Hour	Summary of Events and Information	Remarks and references to Appendices
MARTINSART	22nd May 1916		The transfer of the Ammunition Column of the Brigade to D. Echelon D.A.C. took place. All personnel, equipment, wagons & horses were handed over. The following changes also took place:- D/153 (18 Pdr) was transferred to 154 Bde as C/154. C/154 (4·5 How) " " " 153 Bde. as D/153.	
	23rd		Enemy active during greater part of the day.	
	24th		Situation normal with the exception of Trench Mortars active on R31a.	
	25th		Sniping from Q24 & 3060 was stopped by our guns.	
	26th		Instructional shooting for Officers of 90th Siege Battery. HAMEL and communication trenches in neighbourhood of CHARLES AVENUE shelled by 77mm. MESNIL shelled by 105 m.m. & 77 m.m. guns. Further instructional shooting for Officers of 90th Siege Battery. AVELUY WOOD was shelled by 15·0 m.m. guns. A/153 was bombarded by about 40 rounds of the same calibre. One shell fell close to No.1 gun position the gun being put about a foot. 2 men were wounded.	
	27.		Observation balloon up in direction of GRANDCOURT directing fire on Q27d the greater part of the day.	
	28"		Fairly quiet all day.	
	29"		Q21c. shelled intermittently throughout the afternoon - otherwise quiet.	
	30"		HAMEL heavily shelled by 77 m.m. No item in enemy's artillery appears to have	
	31st		taken place during the month.	

J.W. Barlow? Lt. Col. R.F.A.
Commanding 153rd Brigade R.F.A.

36th Divisional Artillery.

153rd BRIGADE.

ROYAL FIELD ARTILLERY.

JUNE 1916

Army Form C. 2118.

June 1916

153rd Brigade R.F.A. Vol 6
XXXVI

WAR DIARY or INTELLIGENCE SUMMARY

(Erase heading not required.)

Place	Date	Hour	Summary of Events and Information	Remarks and references to Appendices
MARTINSART	1-6-16 2nd		Hostile artillery quiet all day. A few 77mm were sent over into Q17a. r Q24a. Q16 r Q17 were shelled throughout the day by 105mm. also Q23 r Q24 were shelled in the early morning by 77mm.	
	3rd		Hostile Artillery fairly quiet. A few 77mm fell in HAMEL and AUCHONVILLERS Ridge while Q27 r 28 were shelled by a few 105mm. Four heavier calibre shells fell in Q23. (150mm)	
	4th		A fair amount of activity was apparent our front-line being shelled continuously with 77 shrapnel. also Q23 received 6. 105mm.	
	5th		During the day enemy artillery was fairly quiet, about 50. 77mm were fired into Q24a - THIEPVAL WOOD (also returning a share of its own calibre shells. Several 105mm fell in Q16d. During the night of the 5/6 th Bombardment Hostile artillery fire was intense and continued for some considerable time after our own fire had ceased.	
	6th		Slight enemy activity was displayed throughout the day. 77mm shell fire being turned against Q16d. Q27 a, b, r. R.25c	
	7th		105mm guns were active all day on intermittent fire being kept up on Q16 f. Q.H.d. Q.23 a,b. Intermittent shelling 77mm fired on Q 27d.	
	8th		Q.16. 27 r 23 have been suspected to hit from 77mm guns during the day. by 210mm Hows. MAILLY/MAILLET was shelled by 210mm Hows.	
	9th		67 77mm throughout the day on Q.16. 17 r 23. 40. 97mm being fired into Q34 &. Q 23. MESNIL was also shelled during the day. Hostile artillery fairly active, about 40.0. 97mm being fired in to Q34f. Q23. MESNIL was also shelled during the day.	
	10th		Several 105mm were put in Q.16. r Q.28. r 30. Also numerous 97mm were sent over into Q17. Q.23. 25. r. 30 r R.25.	6/12/10/mg
	11th		On the night of 10/11th the enemy heavily bombarded our trenches to the left of HAMEL from 11-45pm Quiet all day. A few 77mm were fired into HAMEL.	
	12th		Hostile arty was again quiet. Several 105mm fell in Q16d.	
	13th		Numerous 77 were again fired into Q16. 23. 17. Q22. 24. 30., r R.31a.	

Army Form C. 2118.

June 1916.

WAR DIARY
INTELLIGENCE SUMMARY
(Erase heading not required.)

153rd Brigade. R.F.A.

Instructions regarding War Diaries and Intelligence Summaries are contained in F. S. Regs., Part II. and the Staff Manual respectively. Title pages will be prepared in manuscript.

Place	Date	Hour	Summary of Events and Information	Remarks and references to Appendices
MARTINSART	14th		R.25a & R.310 & CHARLES AVENUE were shelled by 77 m.m. & 105 m.m. during the day.	
	15th		Normal all day. A few 77 mm were sent over into Q.22.b. Q.17.c & Q.24.a.	
	16th		A few 105 mm shells were fired into Q.16.d & several Trench Mortars fell in Q.24.b.	
	17th		Several rounds of 105 m.m. H.E. fell in Q.16.b. at a very slow rate of fire during & R.25a. the day — otherwise quiet.	
	18th		Throughout the day hostile artillery was fairly active. MESNIL Ridge being shelled by a good number of 105 m.m. who entrance 1/6 JACOB'S LADDER (Q.23.a & CHARLES AVENUE (Q.23.b) received their attention being subjected to 77 gun fire.	
	19th		A few 77 mm shells fell in Q.22.b & Q.23.b.	
	20th		Quiet all day. A few rounds of 15 cm were fired into Q.26.	
	21st		Hostile Artillery active all day. Numerous 77 mm were sent over into Q.24.d Q.17.c & Q.21.a. THIEPVAL WOOD & MESNIL CHATEAU neighbourhood were shelled by guns of small calibre	
	22nd		Normal. A few rounds of 105 m.m. H.E. fired into Q.34.b. Slight enemy activity was displayed throughout the day. Several 77 mm fell in R.25.c. Q.27.a & Q.17.	
	23rd		The Brigade Headquarters moved from MARTINSART to BOUZINCOURT. The lights in trig. ords in the TONRUIUS near MESNIL. Communication to all Batteries & OPs was excellent all wires being buried at an average depth of 2 ft. The Brigade automatically became the Right Group of the 36th Division. The following Batteries	

Army Form C. 2118.

WAR DIARY
INTELLIGENCE SUMMARY.
(Erase heading not required.)

Instructions regarding War Diaries and Intelligence Summaries are contained in F.S. Regs., Part II. and the Staff Manual respectively. Title pages will be prepared in manuscript.

153rd Brigade R.F.A.

Place	Date	Hour	Summary of Events and Information	Remarks and references to Appendices
MESNIL	JUNE 1916. 23rd		Batteries are in the GROUP. A. Battery 153 Brigade R.F.A. B. " " " " C. " " " " D. " " " " A. " 246 " (49th Division. West Ridings Field Artillery.)	
	24th (U Day)		About 50 – 10.5 cm fell in THIEPVAL WOOD & front edge of AVELUY WOOD. Several H.E. shells fell on Q34 & mostly 10.5 cm also several shells of the same calibre fell into MESNIL. Batteries of the GROUP started wire cutting with excellent results from very slow observed fire. Wire cutting was continued in a deliberate manner and Test bursts & barrages on pre-arranged points on the enemy front-were carried out. Enemy very active all day. A large number of 10.5 cm were fired into HAMEL & THIEPVAL WOOD.	
	25th (V Day)		Wire cutting again. In the afternoon a discharge of gas from several points on our front. The Group bombarded in support of this. Tin shells & about 20 lbs 15 cm & around MESNIL Village & about 1000 lbs in THIEPVAL WOOD & area S. of it - mostly 177 mm & 10.5 cm. THIEPVAL WOOD was bombarded by shell of various calibre for about an hour early in the morning. A few 150 cm fell into MESNIL.	
	26th (W Day)		Snipe & Wire cutting.	
	27th (X Day)		Postponed for 48 hours. Hostile Arty more active than during the previous 24 hours. Several 10.5 cm & 15 cm fell in Q28 & d & in Q34 a & b. East of MESNIL was shelled with guns of the same calibre.	
	28th (Y Day)		Wire cutting & a couple of test concentrations. Enemy very active during the day. MESNIL & MESNIL Chateau received much attention from 10.5 & 15 cm. Several 10.5 & 150 cm were fired into HAMEL.	
	29th (Y.1 Day)		Wire cutting. Normally active during the 24 hours. MESNIL, MESNIL Chateau & Q28 & Q34 c were	
	30th (Y.2 Day)			

Army Form C. 2118.

WAR DIARY

INTELLIGENCE SUMMARY.

(Erase heading not required.)

153rd Brigade. R.F.A.

Place	Date	Hour	Summary of Events and Information	Remarks and references to Appendices
MESNIL	JUNE 1916. 30th (Y 2 Day)		Wire cutting. Normally active. During the 24 hours MESNIL MESNIL Station Q 28, Q 34 shelled at different periods by 77 m.m. 10.5 cm & 15 cm. On each night from "U" to "Y" Days inclusive about 100 Rds per gun were fired in order to keep communication trenches in rear. On "W" night the 36th Division state that on account of the plastering of the communication trenches they had had no supplies brought up for 3 days. During the periods of wire cutting 250 rounds per gun were expended for this purpose. Every round was observed & the result was that on "Z" Day (1-7-16) the Infantry, who had all the time been well informed of where the gaps were cut, walked straight through without the slightest difficulty.	

R.E. Thomson
Lt. Col. R.F.A.
Commanding 153rd Brigade R.F.A.

36th Divisional Artillery.

153rd BRIGADE.

ROYAL FIELD ARTILLERY.

JULY 1916

153rd Brigade R.F.A.

WAR DIARY / INTELLIGENCE SUMMARY

July 1916 — 153rd Brigade R.F.A.

Place	Date	Hour	Summary of Events and Information	Remarks and references to Appendices
MESNIL	1st	7.30 AM	Preceded by an intensive Bombardment, an organised and methodical attempt to force the German lines of defence further East was begun along the whole front of 4th Army supported by the 10th French corps on the right, under General Balfourier. The Xth corps, supported by the 8th corps on its left and by the 13th corps on its right, had to establish itself, if possible, on the German 2nd line which on the front runs roughly one kilometre South from GRANDCOURT. On the left of the Xth Corps the 36th Division carried out the task allotted to it without a hitch. Unfortunately, however, the Divisions on its right and left did not meet with the same success. On the right the 32nd Division, the other division of the Xth Corps in front-line found its advance cruelly hampered by the Village of THIEPVAL which, evidently, the defence is mostly contracted from underground as even our most furious bombardment failed to silence the action of the enemy Trench Mortars or to force his infantry into the open. A few machine guns most boldly and skilfully managed, also did much to make any real progress on the part of the 32nd Division impossible for the moment. On our left the 29th Division (of the 8th Corps) even found itself in difficulties. Here again the enemy machine guns played havoc with our Infantry and after some severe fighting the high ground North of the River ANCRE, the main objective of this particular	

Army Form C. 2118.

WAR DIARY
INTELLIGENCE SUMMARY.
(Erase heading not required.)

153rd Brigade R.F.A.

July 1916

Place	Date	Hour	Summary of Events and Information	Remarks and references to Appendices
MESNIL	1st		produced division, still remained in enemy hands. The ill-luck of these two divisions soon spelt danger for the advanced elements of the 36th Division. These had gone forward further than was at first intended & were in danger of being cut off. The penetration of the high ground North of the River ANCRE enabled the enemy to enfilade the leading battalions, & the village of ST. PIERRE DIVION, on the South side of the ANCRE, began to harass our infantry in the same way as THIEPVAL Village showed advance to the 32nd Division. To maintain themselves in such a forward position under these circumstances was impossible and by 8pm nearly all our remaining infantry had been withdrawn to our old front line; a small garrison, whose exact whereabouts was not known, still remained within portions of the enemy trenches to their previous occupants. Our losses were fairly heavy but we had the compensating glory of capturing 600 prisoners most of whom surrendered, given a little more leave on the flanks, the gallantry of our infantry was such that the end of the day would have seen the front line of the Xth Corps on the line LE MOUQUET FARM – GRANDCOURT. The 49th Division in Army Reserve was in immediate support of the 36th Division and by nightfall arrangements had been made for its infantry to replace ours on the line. The arming, or the time of writing to pass under the command of the C.R.A. 49th Division. A.D.S.S./Forms/C. 2118. Support & min. Bombing & rifle fire going on the Our infantry being drawn from Front–	left
2nd				

153rd Brigade RFA. 3

WAR DIARY
INTELLIGENCE SUMMARY
(Erase heading not required.)

Army Form C. 2118.

July 1916

Place	Date	Hour	Summary of Events and Information	Remarks and references to Appendices
MESNIL	2nd		Left flank of this advanced party.	
	3rd		Quiet all day.	
	4th		Quiet. Heavy rain.	
	5th		Shooting going on at Q 24 & A 19. Enemy artillery active firing on MESNIL, AVELUY WOOD, THIEPVAL WOOD & AUTHUILLE – 77 m/m, 105 m/m, 150 m/m & 120m Hows. Laboursatory shells used.	
	6th		Much movement near CRUCIFIX, men seen in full kit & packs moving along the intersecting line in front of above.	
	7th		Parties of enemy from 4-20 men each seen carefully exploring portion of their trenches evacuated by our infantry today.	
	8th		Considerable transport seen moving along the IRLES – GREVILLERS Road. Both ways. Much movement of enemy fully equipped with packs & helmets in the front & support lines to N of the NE 8. Enemy Red X parties out – MESNIL CHATEAU heavily shelled.	
	9th		Nothing of importance happened.	
	10th			
	11th		MESNIL CHATEAU & THIEPVAL WOOD shelled intermittently with different calibres. 3mm gun on lt commenced a bombardment a hostile balloon rose quickly from behind THIEPVAL the light being exceptionally favourable for observation.	
	12th		Brigade moved to HEDAUVILLE (Wagon Lines) & FORCEVILLE	
HEDAUVILLE	13th		Brigade rested at HEDAUVILLE awaiting orders to march	
FORCEVILLE	14th		Brigade marched to GROUCHES	
	15th		— to AUBROMETZ.	

153 Brigade RFA

Army Form C. 2118.

WAR DIARY
or
INTELLIGENCE SUMMARY

(Erase heading not required.)

4   July 1916

Place	Date	Hour	Summary of Events and Information	Remarks and references to Appendices
	16th		Brigade marched to ANVIN	
	17th		— — THÉROUANNE.	
	18th		— — BONNINGUES-LES-ARDRES	
	19th		— — EBBLINGHEM	
	20th		Brigade rested at EBBLINGHEM	
	21st		Orders received for Brigade to go into action. Brigade marched to ROUGE CROIX. Put up for the night.	
	22nd		Continued march to NEUVE EGLISE – Brigade relieved the 24th Divisional Artillery.	
NEUVE EGLISE	23rd		H.Q. 153rd Brigade RFA became H.Q. of Right Group	
	24th		Very quiet on the front.	
	25th		Nothing of importance happened	
	26th		Enemy artillery fairly active	
	27th		Quiet	
	28th		Normal Trench Warfare	
	29th		Aircraft active. Quiet	
	30th		Normal Artillery fire	
	31st		Hostile Artillery quiet	

R.L. Thomson
Lt Col RFA
Commandt 153 Bde RFA

Army Form C. 2118.

WAR DIARY or INTELLIGENCE SUMMARY
(Erase heading not required.)

August 1916. 153rd Brigade R.F.A.

Instructions regarding War Diaries and Intelligence Summaries are contained in F. S. Regs., Part II. and the Staff Manual respectively. Title Pages will be prepared in manuscript.

Place	Date	Hour	Summary of Events and Information	Remarks and references to Appendices
T.21.d.2.1	1st August		Normal Trench warfare. "A" & "B" Batteries cut wire.	
	2.		Hostile Artillery active. Trenches 134 & 135 shelled by Trench Mortars	
	3.		Enemy aeroplanes during the day flew over our positions – driven off by our A.A. guns. T.M.s again active firing on Trenches 141 & 142 apparently from direction of ONTARIO FARM.	
	4.		Wire cut at U.20.80.63. Situation throughout the day quiet. M.G.s active during the night.	
	5.		Two Observation Balloons up all day. Kite Balloon seen – bearing from T.18.b.55.55 – 128°.	
	6.		Quiet all day	
	7.		Hostile Artillery fire normal. Enemy aircraft active afternoon & evening	
	8.		T.M.s very active. Enemy observation balloon seen at a bearing 70° magnetic from O.P. T.18.b.6.9	

August 1916   Army Form C. 2118.

WAR DIARY
INTELLIGENCE SUMMARY
(Erase heading not required.)

153rd Brigade R.F.A.

Place	Date	Hour	Summary of Events and Information	Remarks and references to Appendices
T.21d.2.1.	9th Aug		Situation normal. Trenches 134, 135 fired on by T.Ms	
	10		Wire cut at U.2a.3.2. Enemy commenced to T.M. Trenches 134 & 135 from LA PETITE DOUVE from U.2a.9.8 in the afternoon. Our Howitzers (D.153) retaliated.	
	11		Rifle grenade fire & T.Ms active – otherwise normal	
	12		Quiet. We bombarded Trench Tramway during the night.	
	13		Hostile Artillery fairly active. Night Bombardment of Trench Tramway continued.	
	14		Below the normal. Nothing of importance happened	
	15		Quiet. Group concentration tests were carried out. Snipers post observed at U.8a.87.41 fired at & much damaged	
	16		Hostile Artillery shelled T.17a 4.3 (C.153) also STINKING FARM during afternoon. 2 Hostile planes over T.11a. – driven off by A.A. guns	
	17		MGs active between 10.30pm & 11.30pm. Kite Balloon observed from O.P. T.15k.9.7 bearing 105° True North	

August 1916.

Army Form C. 2118.

WAR DIARY
INTELLIGENCE SUMMARY
(Erase heading not required.)

153rd Brigade. R.F.A.

Place	Date	Hour	Summary of Events and Information	Remarks and references to Appendices
T.21d.2.1	18	Aug.	Quiet all day - wire cutting at U.2.a.4.1	
	19		Situation below normal - wire cutting continued.	
	20		Hostile artillery quiet. Enemy aeroplanes very active over our positions driven off by A.A. guns.	
	21		Normal all day.	
	22		T.Ms from O.31.c.O.3 & O.31.c.20.9.5 shelled our front line Trenches C.1 & C.2. 2 Observation Balloons up all day - observed from T.11a.50.55. True bearing 34°, 81°.	
	23		T.Ms very active, shelled Trenches 134.135.136. We retaliated on LA PETITE DOUVE. Hostile planes over T.18.b. Heavily fired on by A.A. guns. Enemy search light observed from T.18.b. playing from division of WYTSCHAETE.	
	24		Enemy observation balloon up - observed from T.18.f. 90.95. True bearing 90°.	

Army Form C. 2118.

August 1916.

153rd Brigade. R.F.A.

WAR DIARY
or
INTELLIGENCE SUMMARY
(Erase heading not required.)

Instructions regarding War Diaries and Intelligence Summaries are contained in F. S. Regs., Part II. and the Staff Manual respectively. Title Pages will be prepared in manuscript.

Place	Date	Hour	Summary of Events and Information	Remarks and references to Appendices
T.21.d.2.1	24.		90°. A pigeon was seen from T.18.b. 6.9 flying towards German lines in direction of MESSINES.	
	25.		The O.P. at T.18.b. 7.7½ (B.153) was hit by a 10.5 c.m. How: H.E. shell which broke the outside concrete wall & damaged the slit. The O.P. was unoccupied when hit.	
	26.		Hostile Artillery quiet all day. Working party seen at M.2.a.1.9.	
	27.		Normal. Fresh work observed from O.P.U.6.a. in Trench M.2.d.9.8.	
	28.		About 40. 77 m.m shell & 10 Zubrjohn? shells fell in our area during past 24 hours. T.M.s & M.G.s have been noticeably inactive of late. One aeroplane up over T.18.b. Driven off by A.A. guns.	
	29.		Below normal. Only Field guns firing. Heavy thunderstorm in the afternoon.	
	30.		T.M.s active from O.31.c.0.3 & O.31.c.12.7. Very little Art.y fire. Weather very stormy.	
	31.		We bombarded enemy front line trenches at 7.30 this morning. Hostile Arty has been fairly active shelling the following squares T.22.a, T.18.a,b,c,d, T.17.a,b,c, A.tree	

August 1916

Army Form C. 2118.

WAR DIARY
INTELLIGENCE SUMMARY
(Erase heading not required.)

153rd Brigade. R.F.A.

Place	Date	Hour	Summary of Events and Information	Remarks and references to Appendices
T.21.d.2.1	31		was knocked down close to T.17.a. 4½.3 (L.o.153 position). An armstrong hut was used as a bedroom for 2 Officers was badly damaged & nearly all the Officers Kit destroyed. A gunner of A.153 was injured. T.M's were active to the left of our sector. A hostile machine was over Hill 63 early this morning. Driven off by our A.A. guns. Weather more settled & quite good for observation.	

31-8-16.

W. Thomson
Lieut. RFA
Commanding 153 Bde RFA

September 1916

Army Form C. 2118.

WAR DIARY or INTELLIGENCE SUMMARY
(Erase heading not required.)

153rd Brigade. Royal Field Artillery. Vol 9

Instructions regarding War Diaries and Intelligence Summaries are contained in F. S. Regs., Part II. and the Staff Manual respectively. Title Pages will be prepared in manuscript.

Place	Date	Hour	Summary of Events and Information	Remarks and references to Appendices
MAP. 1/20,000 28.S.W.4 PLOEGSTEERT. T.21.2.1	1st Sept?		Hostile Artillery during past 24 hours below the normal.	
	2nd		Enemy shelled square. T.18.c. T.23 a.b.d. & T.24.a with 10.5 cm Shells; also road in T.12.a with 77 m.m shells during the day. Hostile balloon observed from O.P. T.7 True bearing 73°. Between 6 & 7.30 o'clock this evening 4 enemy planes crossed over our lines but were driven back by our A.A. guns.	
	3rd		Normal all day. A few 77 mm shells were fired into T.17.a & T.18 a.d.r.c. Trench Mortars were active during the afternoon to the left of our sector.	
	4.		Hostile Artillery fairly active. We reported two hostile aeroplanes.	
	5.		Nothing of importance happened throughout the day. Hostile & our own artillery quiet.	
	6.		Normal during the day. At night we bombarded enemy C.T.s & approaches.	
	7.		Below the normal. Enemy does not appear inclined to retaliate for our shelling of last night. Group concentrations carried out on MESSINES SQUARE & all cross roads. Continued bombardment throughout the night.	
	8.		A good deal of transport has been heard round MESSINES the last 2 nights. A false GAS alarm was received from the right of our zone.	
	9.		More active than of late, the enemy replied on Trenches 134 & 135. A pigeon flew over T.18.c 9.8 flying W.S.W. from direction of MESSINES.	

Army Form C. 2118.

September 1916

153 Brigade
Royal Field Artillery

WAR DIARY
INTELLIGENCE SUMMARY.
(Erase heading not required.)

Instructions regarding War Diaries and Intelligence Summaries are contained in F.S. Regs., Part II. and the Staff Manual respectively. Title pages will be prepared in manuscript.

Place	Date	Hour	Summary of Events and Information	Remarks and references to Appendices
T.21.c.2.1	10		One enemy plane up, driven off by our AA guns this morning. We bombarded Target U.4 b.10.60 U.24 8.5.65	
	11		Normal trench warfare	
	12		Very quiet during the last 24 hours	
	13		The 153 Brigade R.F.A. changed positions with 172 Bde R.F.A. We now hold the following positions :— A/153 T.3.6. 60.48 (guns) S.5.6. 30.60 (wagon line) B/153 T.16.d. 63.52 (guns) S.35 a 30.50 (wagon line) C/153 T.17.a. 10.50 " " T.18.b. 61. 49 " D/153 T.18.c. 81.80 " " Headquarters T.15.d. 10.20	
T.15.A.10.20	14		Reorganization of artillery came into force "A" Battery bring bombarded and is near "A" Battery 153 Bde R.F.A. was formed. The Brigade now consists of 3 – 6.18 lbr Batteries and 1. 4.5" Howitzer Battery. To enable the 16 lbr 154 Brigade R.F.A. was distributed. T.Ms have been much more active than usual. Enemy T.M. shells fell on our Trenches in N.36.a.&b. Our T.M. briskly a heavy fire on M.5.6. 00.30. A raid was carried out successfully by the Infantry	
	15		We used – 9th Battn. R.I.R. One German prisoner was taken. Batteries registered new barrage lines. Hostile artillery responded feebly to our bombardment.	
	16		This morning + afternoon very quiet. A morning party observed at N.36.d. 70.70 was dispersed by our fire. One of the enemy were observed to M. Kitchel. Our howitzers obtained 3 direct hits on T.M. at N.11.a. 25.35. Enemy machine guns were very active during last night	
	17			

Army Form C. 2118.

September 1916

153rd Brigade
Royal Field Artillery

WAR DIARY
INTELLIGENCE SUMMARY
(Erase heading not required.)

Place	Date	Hour	Summary of Events and Information	Remarks and references to Appendices
T.15.d.10.20.	19.		Hostile artillery a little more active than it has been for the last few days. A sniper was seen at N.36.d.30.80.	
	20.		Quiet all day.	
	21.		At request of Infantry we retaliated for T.Ms with 18 Pdr & 4.5" Howitzers on ONTARIO FARM. Enemy machine gun & rifle fire active during the night.	
	22.		At 3 o'clock this morning a gun alarm was given, which turned out to be fatal. A working party at N.36.d.30.72 was dispersed by our fire. Otherwhere Baltroon was up at true bearing of 28° seen from T.18.b.70.72.	
	23.		The bombardment carried out by us yesterday was very successful. 3 distinct trenches were made in the enemy's lines & wire in places very much damaged. Enemy retaliation very feebly consisting of 6 minenwerfer & 30. 77mm shells & 6. 10·5mm shells. The only damage done to our parapet was one slight breach. Blue and Buff are reported on the enemy's parapet between T.6.b.95.82 & 21.1.a.20.45. also at N.36.d.40.56.	
	24.		Batteries ent wire at N.36.d.70.05. One enemy plane up (DFW Type) over T.17.a. Drove off.	
	25.		There was a small T.M. strafe on both sides at 8 o'clock this morning. Normal all day.	

Army Form C. 2118.

WAR DIARY
INTELLIGENCE SUMMARY
(Erase heading not required.)

153rd Brigade Royal Field Artillery

September 1916

Place	Date	Hour	Summary of Events and Information	Remarks and references to Appendices
T.15.d.b.20	26.		Hostile T.M. active on front line at U.1.d.80.90 this morning. Very little gun fire on either side during the 24 hours.	
	27.		Hostile Art'y fire much below the average. Owing to rain & mist observation has been difficult. At about 6 pm a German Balloon which had drifted from BAPAUME was brought down at N.31.b central containing 1 Officer who was unwounded & is now a prisoner.	
	28.		Normal all day.	
	29.		Very quiet all day. A/153 fired on working party at N.36.d.59.34 which was dispersed	
	30.		Very little firing on either side. Enemy T.M. active this morning.	

30th Sep 1916

R.G. Thomson.
Lieut. Col. RFA
Commanding 153 Bde RFA

WAR DIARY

INTELLIGENCE SUMMARY.

(Erase heading not required.)

Army Form C. 2118.

Vol 10

October, 1916

153rd Brigade Royal Field Artillery

Instructions regarding War Diaries and Intelligence Summaries are contained in F.S. Regs. Part II. and the Staff Manual respectively. Title pages will be prepared in manuscript.

Place	Date	Hour	Summary of Events and Information	Remarks and references to Appendices
Map Reference 1-20,000 28. S.W.4.	1-10-16		Normal Trench Warfare. Very quiet all day. Hostile plane over T.16. yesterday evening flying very high.	
PLOEGSTEERT T.21.d.2.1	2nd	9 am	Infantry reported Wiring party in front of ONTARIO FARM and at O.31.c.45.56 a large Working party was observed. Both parties were engaged by B.153 with effect. Weather very showery.	
	3rd		Hostile artillery has been slightly active on our front line and round BOYLES FARM during the day. T.M.s active on our front line this morning but owing to rain and mist impossible to see their position.	
		3.20 pm	Working party reported by Infantry at O.31.c.45.50 - engaged by B.153 with effect. Operations difficult owing to rain. Hostile Artillery slightly more active during the last few days. T.M.s also active this afternoon reported firing from N.36.d.50.65 & N.36.2.30.90. Our T.M. retaliated with good effect.	
	4th	7.15 am	Working party reported by Infantry at O.31.c.45.70. Was dispersed by B.153. While Very lights are sometimes discharged from about N.36.d.1.7. These lights are only sent up when our aircraft are about & yesterday the following was noticed. Immediately	

WAR DIARY of INTELLIGENCE SUMMARY

(Erase heading not required.)

October 1916. — 153rd Brigade. Royal Field Artillery.

Army Form C. 2118.

Place	Date	Hour	Summary of Events and Information	Remarks and references to Appendices
	4th		Immediately after the discharge of a Very light at this point two shells were fired at a patrolling aeroplane. They missed their mark and shortly after turned and came back in its tracks. It was not shelled until it reached approximately the same spot as before when once again the Very lights were discharged and the two bursts appeared — correct for line (as they were before) but incorrect for range. It seems clear that these guns are set in a fixed line & fall on observer signals on a Very light directly the aeroplane passes across this line.	
	5th		Everything for a bombardment of our front line between 7 & 8.30 pm kept evening hostile artillery has been normal. At the urgent request of the Infantry we retaliated fairly heavily. TMs active during the bombardment from 7.6.8.30pm 4.10.16. A T.M. has been observed firing from O.31.c.10.10.	
	6th	9 AM	We carried out a combined bombardment with T.M.s & rifle grenades. The parapet of the support line at N.2.a.52.07 has been badly knocked about. After the bombardment smoke was seen issuing from N.36.a.75.75. Normal. Working party observed at O.31.c.45.70 & engaged by B.153 & dispersed. Weather cloudy & very windy. (Observation poor).	7th

7.

Army Form C. 2118.

WAR DIARY
or
INTELLIGENCE SUMMARY.
(Erase heading not required.)

153rd Brigade. Royal Field Artillery.   October 1916.

Place	Date	Hour	Summary of Events and Information	Remarks and references to Appendices
	7*		Germans seen in support trench from N.36.d.71.50. to N.36.d.80.32. apparently driving in stakes as though revetting. Infantry reported that a working party was in support trench U.1a.60.75. Normal day. Visibility good most of the time. Intermittent showers.	
	8*		About 12 shells, 3 of which were "duds", fell at about T.15.d.30.30. Evidently searching for the 60 pdr Battery close by our HQrs position. Men seen passing from O.32.t.25.00 to O.32.t.15.30. Vicinity shelled by our 4.5" Battery. Situation all day fairly quiet.	
	9*		Hostile Arty more active than usual. Also T.M's seen firing from M.1.a.28.67. Gas was successfully discharged on night 8/9*. A strong patrol entered enemy trench & returned with 2 prisoners of 121. Regt. The result of the raid seems very satisfactory. The Infantry report that the wire was well cut & presented no obstacle. Numerous coloured lights were sent up by the enemy after gas was discharged. Men seen digging at T.6.t.82.96 & T.6.t.88.97 also movements at O.32.a.75.20 - suspected dump. Below the normal. A lot of new work is in progress in the way of concrete dugouts or emplacements in enemy front & support lines SE of Mortar Farm. N.36.d.70.25. A party of 8	
	10*	9.30am	Germans seen at N.36.d.96.10 apparently mixing cement for concrete under the supervision of an Officer. B/153 fired & dispersed the party. Several shrapnel bursting right on the party. A party	

2353 Wt. W2514/1454 700,000 5/15 D. D. & L.   A.D.S.S. Forms/C. 2118.

Army Form C. 2118.

WAR DIARY
~~INTELLIGENCE SUMMARY.~~
(Erase heading not required.)

October 1916 — 153rd Brigade R.F.A.

Instructions regarding War Diaries and Intelligence Summaries are contained in F. S. Regs., Part II. and the Staff Manual respectively. Title pages will be prepared in manuscript.

Place	Date	Hour	Summary of Events and Information	Remarks and references to Appendices
	10th		A party was seen repairing trench at N.36.d.30.75 — was fired on and dispersed.	
	11th		Normal. T.12 was shelled in morning by 10.5cm show & 15cm Howrs. 8 Rounds Heavy T.M. fell near Northumberland Road. Several white lights were fired by the enemy during the afternoon. Misty at times. Otherwise shewn good.	
	12th	2 AM.	Another raid was successfully carried out. As soon as our artillery commenced to fire 2 red parachute lights well away from place of bombardment, approximately at N.36.d.15.90 were sent up also 3 twin Very lights were fired in quick succession from MORTAR FARM. At 2.7am the enemy commenced to retaliate — a medium T.M. followed by two aerial shot intervals. From this time onwards a fairly continuous fire of these medium T.M.s was kept up at varying points. At 2.15 a.m. our Stokes guns began to fire extremely rapidly. Almost immediately the enemy put up a rocket bursting with white and green stars. This signal was repeated 8 times at 30 seconds intervals & was evidently a request for artillery support.	
		2.17.	The first enemy shell came over — a 10.5cm — bursting high in the air. The artillery barrage developed quickly & became rather severe, though at no time did there seem to be more than 2 batteries firing — a 10.5cm & a 7cm.	
		2.35.	Raiding party safely back (one casualty, a Sergeant wounded) with 1 prisoner. At no time was	

WAR DIARY of INTELLIGENCE SUMMARY

October 1916
153rd Brigade. Royal Field Artillery

Army Form C. 2118.

Place	Date	Hour	Summary of Events and Information	Remarks and references to Appendices
	12th		Was the enemy retaliation formidable & there was no hostile machine gun fire. (Point of Entry N.36.d.30.70.) During the day artillery fire was normal. Normal. Work in progress around N.1.a.12.80 & N.36.d.75.77	
	13th		Hostile artillery slightly more active. T.M's active (between 7.30 & 10.30 a.m. & again at 11 this morning) New wire strand going on on C.T. at N.36.d.20.90. Trench appears to have been revetted. (O.P.T.9) Enemy seen working at N.36.d.77.43. unlikely revetting Trench. (O.P.T.1)	
		9.30 a.m.	2 germans seen at N.30.d.70.27 both wearing dark grey uniforms with round caps.	
	14th		A 77 m.m. gun firing from behind MESSINES but about 20 shell round and about T.18.b.80.70 early this morning. This afternoon T.6.b.40.20 and our front line in N.1.a was fired on by 10.5 cm. Howitzer which judged by sound seemed to be N.E of MESSINES. A 77mm gun firing from the direction of WARNETON was judged by sound was about against LE ROSSIGNOL. About 15 rounds were fired.	
		11.45 a.m	Our T.M's heavily bombard enemy Trenches in N.8.b. New earth thrown up in C.T. O.32.c.15.08 (O.P.T.1) Working party at O.25.d.85.08. seen from N.36.d.05.45. & another at N.36.d.70.30 seen from O.P.T.1 were both fired on by A. & "C" 153 Bde R.F.A. & dispersed. Weather - windy & cloudy.	
	15th		Visibility fair high & good at times. Visibility fair Situation normal all day. Nothing of importance happened to report.	

Army Form C. 2118.

October 1916.

WAR DIARY
INTELLIGENCE SUMMARY
(Erase heading not required.)

153rd Brigade. Royal Field Artillery.

Place	Date	Hour	Summary of Events and Information	Remarks and references to Appendices
	16th		Hostile Arty more active than usual. Between 10-10 and 10.15 a.m. T.12 & 18 a. were shelled with about 16 rds 10.5 cm. How. True bearing 39° from O.P. T.12 a. (T.18 b 92.74). U.1.a. also received attention with guns of the same calibre. Enemy AA guns active all day. German plane over T.18.b. driven off by our AA gun. 2 pigeons were seen to pass at 11.30 am to the left of O.P. 12 a. (T.18 b. 9274)	
	17th		Below normal all day. A few rounds fell round BOYLES FARM, otherwise hostile fire practically nil. T.Ms were slightly active in the neighbourhood of KRUISSTRAAT CABARET. also in N 36c. Reported the morning that one of our aeroplanes brought down in flames our MESSINES this morning by enemy AA gun	
	18th		Hostile Arty more active than yesterday. A Trench Mortar Bombardment was carried out. yesterday afternoon at 4 p.m. in order to flatten out the enemys front line. Our batteries effectively covered the fire of our T.Ms. The enemy retaliated during with about 50 rounds of 5-9 on our support line round AGNES St during & just after yesterday's bombardment. SPRING WALK also received some attention. A few heavy T.Ms were fired during the bombardment. Our 4.5" Howitzers fired on the emplacement at N.36 d. 9852 in retaliation	
	19th		Enemy artillery has been practically inactive during the past 24 hours. A lot of earth has been thrown up at N 36 d. 85 60. Owing to rain & mist observation very difficult.	
	20th		Except for a little shelling of our front line in T.6.t. & U.1.a. between 7.15 & 8.30 this morning the enemys artillery has been very quiet. MGs were more active than usual during the night	

Army Form C. 2118.

WAR DIARY
INTELLIGENCE SUMMARY
(Erase heading not required.)

October 1916 — 153rd Brigade, Royal Field Artillery

Place	Date	Hour	Summary of Events and Information	Remarks and references to Appendices
	20th		A large working party wearing field grey uniforms was observed at O.31.f.12.75 & dispersed. Enemy aircraft more active today than for some time past. 3 planes were over T.17 N. r. & all were driven off by our A.A. guns. At 2.30 pm a Kite Balloon arose at a true bearing of 35° from N.36.d.0 8.50 & after releasing tollowette it descended. At 3.15 pm another balloon appeared over the MESSINES ROAD at 0.32.U.80.30.	
	21st		Normal during last 24 hours. LEROSSIGNOL received a little attention, beyond that a few shells fell in our area. There has been much aerial activity all day. At 9.15 & 11 am an aeroplane flew over our lines & far in the direction of BAILLEUL. At 12.30 pm a fight took place over the German lines between a hostile plane & one of ours. The enemy machine was driven down in a spinning condition in his own lines. (One of our Kite Balloons was attacked by a hostile plane & brought down in flames. True bearing from T.16.d.63.52. was 206°.) The enemy has his own K.B. flying Box kites apparently from 0.33. True bearing taken from N.36.d.15.50. was 80°. The Kites were raised & lowered frequently. Weather fine & cold. Excellent for observation.	
	22nd		N.36.c. was shelled at 7.25 this morning with 10 cm shells & at 12.15 pm BOYLES FARM was shelled with 7.7 mm Shrapnel. Hostile plane over M.13. at 9.40 this morning driven off by our AA guns. Very little shelling fire during the past 24 hours. Weather cold & fine. Observation good.	

WAR DIARY

INTELLIGENCE SUMMARY

October 1916. — 153rd Brigade Royal Field Artillery

Place	Date	Hour	Summary of Events and Information	Remarks and references to Appendices
	23rd		Quiet all day. A snipers post is suspected at N.36.d.45.63. Several working parties observed, fired on & dispersed by 'A' & 'B' Batteries. 153rd Bde. R.F.A. Weather has been fine all day. Observation difficult at times owing to mist.	
	24th		Nothing to report whatever.	
	25th		Hostile Artillery has been more active today, particularly round about N.2.c & d & N.2.a.T.C. About 12 Heavy T.M. projectiles were dropped in N.36.c.95.80 in retaliation for our Stokes Mortars. Newplanes visible at N.2.a.15.95. Our aeroplanes were active in the early morning. Thereafter during the early part of the day fair. Afterwards too cloudy to remain. Enemy's y.y. an Battery active during this afternoon. A minor bombardment by Y. & 36. T.M. Batty (under the control of O.C. 153 Bde R.F.A.) took place yesterday afternoon with the view to cutting wire at points of Entry chosen for forthcoming raids. Owing to low visibility & trouble with some the object was only partially achieved. However, considerable damage was done to enemy's trench including destruction of a large shelter or dug-out, at MORTAR FARM (N.36.d.7.30). There was very little hostile retaliation. A few 77 emas were put over & One or two Heavy T.M's & a fair number of Light T.M's.	
	27th		Another T.M. bombardment took place yesterday afternoon which was carried out on exactly the same lines	

and

WAR DIARY

INTELLIGENCE SUMMARY.
(Erase heading not required.)

October 1916.   Army Form C. 2118.

153rd Brigade. R.F.A.

Place	Date	Hour	Summary of Events and Information	Remarks and references to Appendices
	27th		and with the same object as the bombardment of the 25th inst. There was very little retaliation. A few heavy T.Ms were fired from a position behind MORTAR FARM (N.36.d.70.30) our trenches N.36.1. & 2 also with 7.7 cm shells & light T.Ms. There were no casualties in personnel. T.M. emplacement is suspected at O.31.c.15.65. Weather windy & dull. Observation poor.	
	28th		Very little hostile fire during today. Any single germans were seen along the line. Hostile T.Ms slightly active between 2.15 & 2.45 this afternoon, probably in retaliation for our T.M. bombardment. Trench mortar thrown up at O.19.d.50.30.	
	29th		This morning our T.M. Battery (Y.36) endeavoured to cut wire at U.1.a.27.68, but owing to high wind accurate shooting was almost impossible. 30 rounds were fired, 7 of which were well placed & others did much damage to parapet & surroundings. The enemy retaliated with 8 rounds of Heavy T.Ms over Trenches U.1.7 & U.1.8. & also a few rounds of Light T.M. & 77 mm gun. These mostly fell in direction of BOYLES FARM near the spot from which our fire originated. No casualties to personnel or equipment. Hostile Arty practically inactive. Yesterday evening our Trenches in U.1.1 were shelled & 12 shells fell in T.3.a. Between 12.15 & 12.45 pm about 9 hostile T.Ms fell in neighbourhood of BOYLES FARM & 2 in Trench T.6.5. Several machine	
	30th		Front line parapet at N.36.d.40.72 & N.36.d.32.70 has been built up. These were seriously damaged by	

WAR DIARY
INTELLIGENCE SUMMARY

October 1916 — 153rd Brigade R.F.A.

Army Form C. 2118.

Place	Date	Hour	Summary of Events and Information	Remarks and references to Appendices
	30th		By our T.M.s. German gun at 019.d.50.00. A sap has been dug & covered with a waterproof sheet running from German front line to N.36.d.05.70. Weather showery & windy. Unfavourable for observation.	
	31st	2:10 a.m.	At 2.10 this morning a Raid was carried out by our Infantry (15th R.I.R.) for which we had arranged to provide covering fire. It was however unsuccessful & no report for our support was received. One of the enemy (a sentry) was believed killed. Infantry casualties were one man killed & one Sergeant wounded. Several working parties were observed during the day & fired on & dispersed. Hostile Arty has been very quiet during the last 24 hours. The new Trench at O.25.b.40.80 has been worked on a good deal lately. It appears to be deep & has been extended 50 yards up the hill. Weather showery. Observation good at intervals.	

1st Novr 1916.

A.F. Thomson
Lieut. Col. R.A.
Commandg. 153rd Brigade R.F.A.

Army Form C. 2118.

WAR DIARY
INTELLIGENCE SUMMARY
(Erase heading not required.)

153rd BRIGADE.
— ROYAL FIELD ARTILLERY. —

Vol XI

NOVEMBER — 1916.

Place	Date	Hour	Summary of Events and Information	Remarks and references to Appendices
MAP. 1-20,000 28. S.W PLOEGSTEERT T21a 20.10	1-11-16		Hostile Artillery was practically inactive. A few scattered rounds of 10·5 cm. and 7·7 cm calibre fell in N.36.c. during the afternoon. 10 Rounds heavy French Mortar fell North of DURHAM ROAD. Visibility poor throughout the day.	
	2nd	Hostile Arty below the normal	all day. Up to noon observation very difficult owing to rain and mist. After noon observation fair	
	3rd		Except for 20 Rounds of 10·5 cm "Boom" which fell in T.6.b. & N.36. & a few rounds of Heavy T.M.s in the vicinity of N.36.c.10.85. the enemy have been quiet. 2 working parties were observed at O.32 a 65·00 & 94 a 40·70. Both were dispersed by our fire. One of our Kite Balloons was seen to break away from its cable at 1·50 p.m & drift from the vicinity of KEMMEL to the N.E.	
		3 p.m	A.T.M. Bombardment arranged previously took place this afternoon, the objective being ts enemy's front	
		3·50 p.m	and support lines between N.36 & 63·30 & T.6.b. 80·95. Our 'A', 'B' & 'C' Batteries co-operated with covering fire. The 107th Stokes Mortar Battery also helped in this shoot. A great many direct hits were observed, numerous Shrapnel & Stokes were destroyed & the material flying high into the air. Other rounds fell into the enemy wire & did considerable damage. The retaliation promised was very little. As	
		4·10 p.m	conditions were normal again. There were no casualties either to personnel or equipment.	
	4th		Hostile Artillery was rather more active today. About 12 rounds 10·5 cm fell in the neighbourhood of our	

Army Form C. 2118.

WAR DIARY
INTELLIGENCE SUMMARY.
(Erase heading not required.)

153rd Brigade. — Royal Field Artillery —

Place	Date	Hour	Summary of Events and Information	Remarks and references to Appendices
	4th		of our H.Q. (T.15.d.10.20) intended for the heavy Battery close by. The bulk of the enemy fire was concentrated on the T. & W. Trenches & seemed to come from batteries at O.34.11&b. & O.33 of which that at O.33 was of 10.5 cm. Howitzer entirely. Enemy's T.M. fired a few rounds at 3.45 pm and was located at O.31.a.30.45 & fired on & silenced by "D/153.	
	5th		Quiet all day. Again the vicinity of our Headquarters was shelled by 15 c.m. H.E. about 30 rounds were fired (unused) this morning no doubt searching for the heavy battery. New work in progress at O.31.c.05. At O.25 to 50.70 a new trench is marked out by a white tape. At O.31.c.5.0 work has progressed. At BIRTHDAY FARM new material is visible resembling girders & pillprops. Several germans were seen during the day. One or two groups were fired on by our artillery & dispersed. A strong conterally wind all day.	
	6th		Hostile Artillery fairly active all day. Apparently they have been searching for the 60 Pdr Battery close to our H.Q. More working parties were seen & dispersed. There is a dug-out with a square aperture visible behind Trench wood screen at O.31.6.48.14. Weather showery. Observation difficult at times	
	7th	Hostile Arty. Normal.	A good deal of work is going on at SLOPING ROOF FARM. It looks as though the farm is being fortified. The T.M. Bombardment arranged for this afternoon took place against MORTAR FARM and the trenches in its vicinity. It commenced at 3 pm. and lasted till 3.30 pm. 2-2" T.M. (Y.36 Batty) & 3 Stokes	

Army Form C. 2118.

November 1916.   153rd Brigade.
                        Royal Field Artillery

WAR DIARY
INTELLIGENCE SUMMARY
(Erase heading not required.)

Place	Date	Hour	Summary of Events and Information	Remarks and references to Appendices
	8.		Stokes Mortars (107 & 2/7 Bde) took part. The effect was excellent - & both types of mortar shot splendidly. Many direct hits were observed on enemy dug-outs, trenches and wire. The new heavy T.M. at O.31.a 30.45 was silenced immediately after it had opened fire. A 77 mm battery started searching for our 2" T.M. position at 3.20 pm firing 12 rounds & then fired 30 more rounds commencing at 3.45 pm. No casualties to personnel or equipment. Visibility fair. Raining most of the day.	
	9.		Below normal. 3 working parties were seen at 10.15 am, 12.5 pm & 12.35 pm near SLOPING ROOF FARM. They wore dark green uniforms. 3 men wearing round caps and grey uniforms were seen at O.31.d 68.37 at 11.5 & 11.45 a.m. They were fired on and dispersed by 16/153'. Hostile aircraft has been more active today than it have been for a long time. Their aeroplanes repeatedly attempted to cross our lines but were driven off each time by our A.A. guns. Work is still in progress at SLOPING ROOF FARM. Weather fine - strong wind good.	
	10.		Hostile Artillery below normal. More activity of enemy planes. They came over our lines as far as T.16 Central & were heavily bombarded by our A.A. guns & driven off. Work is going on in enemy front-line from N.36.d 63.30 - N.36.d 55.60 & he is apparently clearing his trench. Working party was seen near road at O.32.b 19.24 at 11.15 a.m. Fine, hazy during the morning, clear after midday.	

Army Form C. 2118.

November 1916. 153rd Brigade
WAR DIARY Royal Field Artillery.
INTELLIGENCE SUMMARY.
(Erase heading not required.)

Place	Date	Hour	Summary of Events and Information	Remarks and references to Appendices
	11th		Enemy's artillery practically inactive. Except enemy were seen working on his front line from N.36.d.15.80 - N.36.d.60.35 there is nothing to report. Weather fine but very misty.	
	12th		There was little more activity today. Occasional parties of men were seen working along the WYTSCHAETE - MESSINES Road in O.32.c. At 12.50 pm a working party of about 12 men at O.32.d.25.05 were fired on with effect by A/153. Fine misty, observation fair.	
	13th	Artillery	Below the normal all day. A working party was observed in O.T. at O.32.c.35.85. A/153 fired on them effectively. Fine inclined to be misty.	
	14th	Artillery	Slightly more active today. Enemy T.M. have been remarkably quiet for the last few days. Several working parties were seen, fired on and dispersed. Fine observation good.	
	15th		A very successful combined bombardment was carried out this morning by 136 2"T.M.Battery + 107 Stokes Mortar Battery aided by our Batteries with covering fire. The targets were enemy's front trench at U.2.c.60.93 (where it crosses the GABION FARM - MESSINES Road + for a distance of 30 yards on either side - a great deal of work is reported at this point) + T.M + M.G emplacements at T.6.b.88.92 (and one old dug-out close by) N.36.a.60.40 (THE NOSE) N.36.a.48.97. N.30.c.38.47. Zero time was 11-30am. The bombardment lasted one hour. The retaliation proved was practically NIL Total number of rounds fired by enemy 20, consisting of 10 - 10.5 am + 10 - T.M. Many fired	

Army Form C. 2113.

WAR DIARY
of
INTELLIGENCE SUMMARY.
(Erase heading not required.)

November. 1916   153rd Brigade
                                Royal Field Artillery.

Place	Date	Hour	Summary of Events and Information	Remarks and references to Appendices
	15		direct hits were observed on enemy trenches & the wire was much knocked about. Portions of dug. outs at T.6 b.8.8 9.2 were blown into the air. 40 Rounds of 2" T.Ms were fired on MORTAR FARM and just South of it. There were no casualties to personnel or equipment. Weather fine. Observation good.	
	16		Hostile artillery practically inactive all day. A aircraft sniper's post is suspected at N.36 d. 4.8 6.1. Several men were seen digging at O.31 b. 50.10 & O.32 b. 15.05. At 10.30 am an enemy machine appeared over German lines but was driven off by our AA guns.	
		10 pm	A raid on the enemy trenches on the left sector was carried out this evening by the 109th Infantry Bde very successfully, the raiders covered by 4 batteries & parties of enemy were N.30.c. 50.08 – 50.18 – 48.28 and 41.44. Only 'A' Battery of this Brigade took part, by barraging with 4 guns from N.36 b. 20.88 to N.36 b. 11.98 & N.30 d. 13.05 (beginning of hedge) – N.30 d. 04.15. Numerous german wire killed & prisoners taken of the 104th & 134th Regts. The raiders remained in enemy trenches over an hour. Our own casualties were slight. (8 men killed & 12 wounded) Weather fine, cold & misty.	
	17		Hostile artillery below the normal. Enemy T.Ms. fairly active after our bombardment which was carried out this morning on N.36 d. 65.15 to 150 yards North including MORTAR FARM by 136. 2" T.M.Bty in conjunction with 107 Stokes Mortar Bty. It lasted half an hour. All guns shot very well. Many	
		10.15 am		

Army Form C. 2118.

WAR DIARY
or
INTELLIGENCE SUMMARY.
(Erase heading not required.)

153rd Brigade
Royal Field Artillery

November 1916

Place	Date	Hour	Summary of Events and Information	Remarks and references to Appendices
	17th		Many direct hits were obtained on the enemy's wire and trenches which were observed to be badly knocked about by the Bombardment; also the Trench Tramway which runs through MORTAR FARM must have been considerably damaged as pieces of rail were seen to be shot high in the air. No casualties to personnel or equipment.	
	18th	Hostile Arty.	About the normal all day. At 9.15 a.m. a small working party was observed at N.36.d.18.85 & dispersed by B/153. Observation poor.	
	19th		Hostile Artillery quiet. T.Ms were active in morning & afternoon; several T.Ms fell in N.36.d. The 18 Pdr Batterys & 4.5 Howitzer Batty of our Group (CENTRE) opened fire and silenced them. 5" german were seen working along Trenches at O.19.d.65.33. They disappeared into a small shed which is apparently built into the railway cutting about this point. Weather bad & misty.	
	20th	Hostile Arty. Normal.	Several parties of germans seen during the day. Work is in progress at O.31.b.10.60. New shelters have been driven in here & wire netting put up. Weather fine. Visibility poor.	
	21st	Hostile Arty. Below the normal.	Nothing of importance happened to report.	
	22nd		Hostile Artillery - nil. Working party seen at N.36.d.18.85 repairing trench. Was fired on by "A/153" & dispersed. Cold & misty. Visibility very bad.	
	23rd		Very quiet all day. Working party reported by Infantry at 8 am at W.1.a.26.70. Fired on by "B/153" and dispersed.	

Army Form C. 2118.

WAR DIARY
or
INTELLIGENCE SUMMARY.

(Erase heading not required.)

153rd Brigade
— Royal Field Artillery. —

November 1916

Place	Date	Hour	Summary of Events and Information	Remarks and references to Appendices
	24th	10.15 am	The enemy opened fire with T.Ms on our front line. 5 at least were observed in action.	
		10.50 pm	An "S.O.S" Left batt. was received at 10.50 pm. All Batteries switched 1 battery Night Lines left & fired as laid down till the "STOP" signal was received from 36th Div Arty	
	25th		Too wet and misty for observation	
	26th	9.30 am	At 9.30 this morning an enemy aeroplane flew very low over T.15. It was engaged by our AA guns. Either because it was hit or as a ruse to make the guns cease firing it volplaned down till it was about 20 yards above the ground below the top of the trees near B/153's position at T.16.d flying parallel to the ground. The pilot then put the engine at full speed and forcing its nose up clears the trees and at off toward Hill 63. Here, it only just cleared the crest passing over T.18.c at a height of 75 to 100 feet. It flew over the trenches but was not engaged by rifle or MG fire till it was over the German lines, owing to its being mistaken for one of our own. As soon as it was well over the hostile trenches it rose and went out of sight over the ridge still flying low. The look-out man and the BSM of B/153 both agree in saying that this machine bore our markings underneath the wings & was flying a pennant at its tail. Other observers noticed an "Iron Cross" on the side of the machine. The general opinion is that the descent was due to engine failure, or loss of petrol, as the engine seemed to fail after the plane had risen a certain distance & the pilot had to volplane to get up speed and to get the engine going again. The engine again stopped at ST. QUENTINS CABARET. Observers near	

Army Form C. 2118.

WAR DIARY
~~INTELLIGENCE SUMMARY.~~
(Erase heading not required.)

153rd Brigade
Royal Field Artillery

Place	Date	Hour	Summary of Events and Information	Remarks and references to Appendices
November 1916	26th		near PETIT PONT say that the pilot was brought to & that the observer in the seat behind was leaning over & guiding the machine & that it was so low that stones were thrown at it. Others witnessed say that the machine contained 2 passengers besides the pilot, & that no more could be seen in the plane hanging over the side apparently dead. Two working parties were dispersed by 2 g. our Batteries.	R.E. Thomas Lieut R.F.A. Commands 153rd Brigade R.F.A
	27th		A little T.M. activity. Several germans were seen during the day and one working party which was dispersed by one of the Batteries. A hostile balloon was up on a true bearing of 27° from O.P.T.B. and two hostile planes came over T5 & T6. Weather fine down stream fair.	30th Nov 1916
	28th	1-30pm to 3.15pm	No observation unreportable owing to a thick fog which completely hid the two hostile front lines from one another for the greater portion of the day. This enabled NO MAN'S LAND to be entered in daylight - all along the sector & infantry wiring parties were out. Nothing to report owing to thick mist.	
	29th			
	30th		Hostile Artillery fairly active all day. We carried out a very successful T.M. Bombardment at 2pm. 12 Stokes Mortars & 9.2" T.M. took part, covering fire was provided by the Batteries of 153 Bde RFA, D/171, & the detached section of B/171/3. D/171/2 & the portion bombarded was the support line from N36d9500 to 70/70. The shooting was very accurate, much material revetments & parapet being blown up in to the air. 3 T.M's (TOR.TIN & TAPE) retaliated a little but were finished by our Batteries. Owing to mist no great observation was possible.	

Wt. W2344/1454 700,000 5/15   D.D.&L.   A.D.S.S. Forms/C.2118.

Army Form C. 2118.

153rd Brigade
Royal Field Artillery

WAR DIARY or INTELLIGENCE SUMMARY

(Erase heading not required.)

Instructions regarding War Diaries and Intelligence Summaries are contained in F. S. Regs., Part II. and the Staff Manual respectively. Title Pages will be prepared in manuscript.

December 1916

Vol 12

Place	Date	Hour	Summary of Events and Information	Remarks and references to Appendices
MAP 1/20000 28 SW	1-12-16		One T.M. (T.M.) was reported active by the Infantry & was effectively dealt with by 'A' 'C' & 'D' Batteries. Weather fine.	
PLOEGSTEERT	2nd		A little artillery activity on front system by a 7.7 cm and a 10.5 cm gun — in all about 20 rounds in afternoon. Observation impossible owing to mist.	
T.21.d. 20.10.	3rd		Hostile 10.5 cm How'r active in morning searching from T.5 on to T.6.6. About 35 rounds in all. Weather fine, too misty for observation.	
	4th		N.36.c was shelled by 10.5 cm shells in the morning & a bomber battery was turned on strongly. A german plane attempted to cross our lines but was driven back by our AA guns. Weather fine, observation fairly good in morning.	
	5th		Enemy artillery more active than usual. A.153 & B.153 were shelled by 10.5 cm 4.2" H.E. in air and on graze but no damage was done though one pit was almost hit by three in succession. One TM was active in the morning (T.O.R.) & was punished. Several germans were seen at O.31.d.55.92, one was wearing a white band round his arm. 2 others at N.36.d.62.25 were wearing khaki grey helmets & two were seen at O.19.d.9070 carrying firewood.	

2449 Wt. W14957/M90 750,000 1/16 J.B.C. & A. Forms/C.2118/12.

Army Form C. 2118.

WAR DIARY
or
INTELLIGENCE SUMMARY

(Erase heading not required.)

153rd Brigade
Royal Field Artillery

December 1916

Place	Date	Hour	Summary of Events and Information	Remarks and references to Appendices
Trench Mortars	5.12.16		Weather fine after 9 AM, Visibility good.	
	6th		A T.M. Bombardment was carried out in the morning by Y.36 a' Battery & 107 B.do Stores Mortars from 7 AM – 7.25 AM (8 guns in all) 94 + 300 rounds were fired respectively. The enemy front line and wire was badly damaged & judging from the screams & calls in the trenches must have caught him when the trenches were full of men. Two hostile T.M.s were active in reply (T.M & T.R.P.B) but were quickly diminished. A working party of 7 men were seen to leave the enemy front line by the C.T. at N.36.d.25.70. Weather fine but visibility bad.	
	7th		A T.M. Bombardment was carried out at 7.30 AM – 7.35 AM by Y.36 2" T.M.Battery & 107 Stokes Mortar Battery (8 guns in all) 95 + 300 rounds were fired respectively. Enemy retaliation was fairly feeble, two T.M.s (TRUE & TITUS) were active but were punished severely. Weather fine observation even from front line impossible owing to mist.	
	8th		Very slight hostile artillery on our front line. T.O.81 was active in afternoon & was punished by 18 Pdrs & 4.5 How. Weather fine but too misty for observation	
	9th		Artillery more active than usual. "TITU" was active & was punished by a' & D 153 Batteries. 2	

WAR DIARY / INTELLIGENCE SUMMARY

Army Form C. 2118.

153rd Brigade Royal Field Artillery

December 1916.

Date	Hour	Summary of Events and Information	Remarks
9th		2 men were seen carrying sandbags at 9 am on the road at O.26.a.55.01 going towards 4 HUNS FARM. Weather rainy & misty. Visibility bad.	
10th		Artillery more active than usual. WULVERGHEM, HILL 79, & trenches in N.36 & T6 were intermittently shelled by a 15 cm Howitzer & a 77 mm gun. Smoke was observed at O.31.b.65.97 & O.31.b.21.70. Walker Built & inclined to rain. Visibility bad. Enemy artillery active. WULVERGHEM & Front-Line T6 1 & 2 shelled with 105's & 77 mm. "TIN & TAPE" were active at 12.15 pm and were engaged.	
11th		Quiet. Visibility very bad owing to mist & snow.	
12th		Quiet. Visibility very bad.	
13th		T.M. activity in WULVERGHEM sector - otherwise quiet.	
14th		A pre-arranged T.M. Bombardment was carried out in the PETITE DOUVE SECTOR. Y.26 & 107 Steen Akerun hook "Park". It commenced at 10.30 am & by 10.40 a.m. were blown in the Enemy's parapet, much material, french boards &c were thrown into the air. A direct hit was scored on to a bomb store at U.8.6.1.8 & a tremendous explosion took place. Germans were seen running through the smoke getting out of the front line trench & running back to the rear soon after the bombardment commenced. The enemy retaliation	

Army Form C. 2118.

WAR DIARY
or
INTELLIGENCE SUMMARY
(Erase heading not required.)

153rd Brigade Royal Field Artillery

December 1916

Place	Date	Hour	Summary of Events and Information	Remarks and references to Appendices
	15th		retaliation was swift and heavy consisting of 105 mm, 77 mm & T.M.'s. He located our T.M's & caused casualties to both 62" & Stokes. The fire of the 2" were very accurate in spite of casualties, & great gallantry and devotion was shown by all ranks. The enemy retaliated with heavy Minenwerfer & 105 mm How'r on AGNES STREET and Front Line near Lft Company of Lft Battn. and a direct hit from former was scored on the Sunken trench. ½ - 9.2 How: 2 - 6" How: & 21 - 18 pdrs took part firing on Support line between U.8.b 40.45 & W.8.b 06.89. 700 rounds of shrapnel were used. 18 Pdrs fired HE.	
	16th		Nothing to report. Minenwerfer Germans sentries &c were seen in front trench near N2b.b.85.32.	
	17th		Enemy T.M. active to N. of our sector. A few rounds fell near DURHAM Road & the T.M. men engaged. Modest hast.	
	18th		LE ROSSIGNOL & neighbourhood was shelled by 105 mm Batty which was engaged by our heavy artillery. Ft. OSBORNE Bks was shelled by a 105 batty & a direct hit was scored. A big explosion was heard about 2.30 pm & a large column of smoke was seen apparently in O.26.	
	19th		A ka'm quiet. Probably very bad most of the day. 4 germans were seen at N.36.d.53.82. "Tom" which had been removed from the active list has again been firing & the emplacement	

Army Form C. 2118.

WAR DIARY
INTELLIGENCE SUMMARY
(Erase heading not required.)

Place: 153rd Brigade Royal Field Artillery
Date: December 1916

Date	Hour	Summary of Events and Information	Remarks and references to Appendices
19th		emplacement has evidently been repaired since our last bombardment. AGNES St & back areas near WULVERGHEM were shelled in morning. Enemy retaliated on AGNES St for a T.M. Bombardment by division on left with 105 + m/m m/m fire - no TMs fell in our sector - Showed in afternoon	
20th		WULVERGHEM shelled in [ ] afternoon by 15 c.m. Our artillery fired on O.31.c.80.73 & where activity was observed where activity was observed. Weather fine	
21st		WULVERGHEM & front line again occasionally shelled with 150 m.m. shells. Weather rainy	
22nd		A working party was seen at O.31.6.04.73 & dispersed with casualties. Numerous gunmen were seen. Visibility not very good. Weather rainy & misty	
23rd		Two german arm. on road O.19.d.1.3 carrying planks at 2.15 pm. A gas attack was carried out in front of 10th & 18th R.I.R. The discharge took place at 5 pm (Zero time) at which time the wind was S.W. & 15 m.p.h. The cloud kept low & did not disperse. Enemy made no sign for 6 mins when 2 orange rockets were sent up opposite the WULVERGHEM Sector & from MESSINES. Enemy retaliated with 150 m.m. shrap. for a considerable time after the discharge. At 2.30 plus 2 hours 2 patrols were sent out - but they found the enemy standing-to & could not proceed	

Army Form C. 2118.

WAR DIARY or INTELLIGENCE SUMMARY

(Erase heading not required.)

Place: 153rd Brigade Royal Field Artillery
December 1916

Date	Hour	Summary of Events and Information	Remarks and references to Appendices
23rd		No further than the German wire. Both parties were fired upon and our received showers of bombs. 3 slight casualties were suffered in these 2 patrols.	
24th		In morning a few 15 cm Howr shell burst in air near 60 pdr battery at T21.d.33.99. T.U.t. were active & heavily trenmated. A morning party were seen at O.31.d. 05.70 & was disposed by our artillery. Hostile aeroplanes very active in morning T & were engaged by AA guns & our planes. Visibility very good.	
25th		"TAPE" "TITUS" & "TIN" active & engaged. 4 men were seen carrying timber at HELL FARM and 6 men were seen on road at O.19.d.1.3 carrying parcels & at 2.30pm. Visibility good. Between 4.30 & 6.40 pm about 180 rounds percussion H.E. were fired at the 60 pdr Battery at T.21.b.38.99. The greater proportion were extra. The main point of impact being in the mash field judged by a group of 40-50 rounds between the points T.12.b.29.48 & 45.83. One direct hit was scored on the ammunition recess of an unoccupied gunpit & a hut at T.21.t-18.90 was damaged. 2 horses were wounded. Otherwise no damage was sustained. Fuzes were recovered but in every case the lower ring is blown off & the length of fuze is unknown. The first to DopH 2 by BRIG Sp.16 & an L is stamped on the fuzing.	

Army Form C. 2118.

WAR DIARY
of
INTELLIGENCE SUMMARY
(Erase heading not required.)

153rd Brigade. Royal Field Artillery

December 1916.

Place	Date	Hour	Summary of Events and Information	Remarks and references to Appendices
	25th		Today of the first. There were at least 2 guns in action — calibre 15 cm How: & were firing from direction of O.27 or O.34. Visibility fairly good.	
	26th		A few rounds 150 mm How: fell in same place as yesterday. At 3.30 pm 2 german planes came over & registered for 2 batteries. About 150 rounds were fired, presumably at the former at T.16.d.4040 & T.16.d.3080. One direct hit on the former was scored, the rest of the rounds a mixture of 10 cm & a few 15 cm fell in the field N. of the latter.	
	27th		2 Hostile planes up over MESSINES observing for 10.5 cm battery at 3 pm. Visibility bad. Artillery quiet.	
	28th		Artillery active on Front Line in afternoon. Weather wet & wind high	
	29th		Working party of about 6 men seen near house at O.19.d. 70.25 — fired at and dispersed.	
	30th		2 shots were obtained on the house, & several germans ran out into the open. Weather fine. Visibility good.	
	31st		4.5 pm. Hostile plane up over T.17 a apparently observing for battery which was firing at T.17 a. Weapons were arriving at A/19/2: position at the time & it is conceivable that they had been "spotted" by the aeroplane. 10.5 cm & 15 cm Regular very active. — About 250 rounds falling in vicinity of	

Army Form C. 2118.

WAR DIARY
INTELLIGENCE SUMMARY
(Erase heading not required.)

December 1916.

153rd Brigade Royal Field Artillery

Place	Date	Hour	Summary of Events and Information	Remarks and references to Appendices
	31st		of N.36.1. to 3. "TIN" "TUB" "TAPE" "TITUS" & "SISTER" were reported active & punished At. O.31.f. 50.12. new earth & a screen have appeared & 16 mm wire seen there. Weather fine. Visibility fair.	

31st December 1916.

W. Thomson
Lt. Col. RFA.
Commanding 153rd Brigade, RFA.

Army Form C. 2118.

WAR DIARY
of
INTELLIGENCE SUMMARY

153rd Brigade
Royal Field Artillery

WF/13

JANUARY 1917

Place	Date	Hour	Summary of Events and Information	Remarks and references to Appendices
MAP. 1-20,000. 28. SW.	1st		Artillery and Trench Mortars quiet. Weather fine. Visibility good. In reply to our Artillery Bombardment to the North of our sector the enemy sent over about 30-77cm Fd gun. H.E. on to NEUVE EGLISE at midnight.	
PLOEGSTEERT. T.21.d.20.10.	2nd		A combined bombardment was carried out on "NUTMEG RESERVE" 290 rounds being fired by the 2" Trench How"s & 9 rounds by heavy T.M.s Considerable damage was done to the enemy's trenches. The enemy's retaliation was very slight consisting chiefly of 77mm shrapnel, a few rifle grenades, and light Trench Mortars. "TOM" "TITUS" & "SISTER" were active on N.36.I. & 2. Our casualties were 5 men wounded by 77mm shrapnel. We had 'planes up observing during this bombardment. Weather fine. Visibility good.	
	3rd		15 cm. How active during the day. Weather fine. Visibility poor.	
	4th		"A.153" was heavily shelled by 10 & 15 cm Howitzers during the morning. 2 direct hits were obtained, one dug-out being blown in. The shell used by the 10 cm How was a "LANGE F.H.Gr." Visibility fair.	
	5th		Artillery and Trench Mortars active. A working party was observed at 10.14 am & fired at by "A/153". Several hostile planes were up, but only one crossed our lines, flying over T/8	

WAR DIARY

JANUARY 1917

153rd Brigade, Royal Field Artillery

Army Form C. 2118.

Place	Date	Hour	Summary of Events and Information	Remarks and references to Appendices
over T/8	5th		Weather fine. Visibility good. Artillery less active than usual. A working party observed at O.31.t. 00.80 at 9-10 AM & fired at by "A/153". New work (A frames, etc.) is visible at N.2.a.10.90 & fired at by "B/153.	
	6th		Weather showery & misty. Visibility bad.	
	7th		At 4 AM the enemy bombarded our front and support trenches between SPRING WALK and DURHAM ROAD and on the 16th Div: Front with Howitzers and T.M's stopping at 4.45 AM. About 150 10.5 cm shells fell in our area and much damage was done to material. An "S.O.S" signal was sent up at 4.22 AM by the 16th Divn. The enemy raided our trenches at 4.45 AM entering at N.36.a.5.3 & possibly N.36.c.83.95. 2 of the 16th Divn were missing & several casualties were suffered. Our Division offered 6 casualties. As the raiders left the trenches a Lewis gun opened fire on them and the patrol leader was observed to fall, but he was taken into the German lines. There was much artillery activity on both sides on the right portion of the Divn in the afternoon and BOYLES FARM was shelled. At 3.15 PM a 10.5 cm How. Batty (either that at O.27.b.09.20. or O.27.c.30.11) where flash was distinctly seen, fired 12 rounds at the O.P. at T.18.b.50.60. While our planes were flying low over the lines, a hostile plane darted down from some clouds and	

WAR DIARY or INTELLIGENCE SUMMARY

153rd Brigade. Royal Field Artillery

Army Form C. 2118.

JANUARY 1917.

Place	Date	Hour	Summary of Events and Information	Remarks and references to Appendices
	7th		and machine-gunned on our planes. The petrol tank was set on fire and the plane cut off back coming safely in T.3. The pilot, a Sergeant, was badly burnt & the observer, an officer who was practically unhurt, stood out on the wings spraying him with the fire extinguisher. Weather fine. Visibility poor.	
	8th		"A.153" was again shelled between 11 AM and 1 pm by 10 & 15 cm Howitzers and again between 2.30 pm and 5.30 pm. About 300 shells were fired, mostly over - either on the road or in the fields beyond. The proportion of "duds" was very small considering the wet state of the ground. At 1.30 pm 2 hostile planes came over the position & a few rounds were burst in the air. 2 T.M.s were active and punished. A working party was observed at 3.15 pm at O.31.b.65.04 and was dispersed by "C.153". Hostile artillery inactive. About 20 rounds 10.5 cm Howitzer fell at the East end of NEUVE EGLISE. A combined Artillery and T.M. Bombardment was carried out by the 16th Divn between 7.30 and 8.45 AM. In retaliation a few T.M. bombs and several 77 mm and 105 mm shells fell on the left portion of our sector. Our T.M.s and artillery replied vigorously.	
	9th		A new C.T. is being dug between U.2.a 50.20 to U.2.a 26.30. Weather showery. Visibility fair.	

WAR DIARY / INTELLIGENCE SUMMARY

Army Form C. 2118.

153rd Brigade Royal Field Artillery

JANUARY 1917

Place	Date	Hour	Summary of Events and Information	Remarks and references to Appendices
	10th		A few 10.5 cms fell at East edge of NEUVE EGLISE. Between 7.45 AM and 8.30 AM our trenches N.36/4 were bombarded. R.E. Farm, SURREY LANE and LE ROSSIGNOL were also shelled. 2 T.Ms very active in morning and punished. At about 3.30 p.m. 6 hostile planes crossed our lines, flying towards DRANOUTRE. 2 of them attracted attention by diving and circling over NEUVE EGLISE at a height of about 1,000 feet. A second flew towards BAILLEUL and was engaged by our AA guns. Another one, keeping hidden in the clouds, reached DRANOUTRE and suddenly darting down machine gunned our observation balloon, setting it on fire and destroying that once. Two men in parachutes were observed to descend to the ground. The planes then returned and were engaged by our AA guns, but with no success, although they were flying very low. They were pursued by one of our planes, who was easily outdistanced - and regained their own lines. Once there, 2 of them continued to dive and circle over the front line with no opposition. Weather fine. Visibility good.	
	11th		Hostile Artillery and T.Ms very inactive all day. Weather snowy and dull. Visibility very bad.	
	12th		Hostile Artillery and T.Ms below normal. Smoke seen at hedge corner. O.31.c.30.40 also at house O.19.d.70.18; also at 1st line M.2.a.13.78 where the parapet is made up largely of blue	

Army Form C. 2118.

WAR DIARY
INTELLIGENCE SUMMARY.
(Erase heading not required.)

JANUARY 1917.

153rd Brigade
Royal Field Artillery

Instructions regarding War Diaries and Intelligence Summaries are contained in F.S. Regs., Part II and the Staff Manual respectively. Title pages will be prepared in manuscript.

Place	Date	Hour	Summary of Events and Information	Remarks and references to Appendices
	12th	11-30 pm	Blue Very and was fired at by "B/153" 10 rounds – 10 or 15 cm Hows. fell in NEUVE EGLISE at 11-30 pm	
	13th		Hostile artillery and T.M's inactive. Weather snow and sleet. Visibility very poor.	
	14th		Machine guns active on both sides. Wiring parties out. A hostile wiring party was observed at N.36.d.75.20 at 4 pm and dispersed by "A/153".	
	15th		Cold and very misty. Visibility very bad.	
	16th		Weather cold and misty. Visibility poor.	
	17th		"TITUS" active and punished. Weather fine and misty. Visibility fair. An artillery bombardment was carried out at 4-50 pm, in order to catch enemy relieving, lasting 10 minutes on support lines & C.T's West of MESSINES. Weather – snowing, visibility bad.	
	18th		2 fresh T.M's active firing near R.E. FARM — about 50 rounds fell. These have been allotted the names "TART" (N.36.b.25.89) and "TURK" (N.36.b.35.35.) Weather snowing and sleeting. Visibility poor.	
	19th		"TART" and "TURK" active and punished. Smoke seen at dug-outs at O.31.f.50.90 & fired at by "B/153". Weather fine and cold. Visibility fair.	

Army Form C. 2118.

JANUARY 1917

153rd Brigade Royal Field Artillery

WAR DIARY / INTELLIGENCE SUMMARY

(Erase heading not required.)

Instructions regarding War Diaries and Intelligence Summaries are contained in F. S. Regs., Part II. and the Staff Manual respectively. Title pages will be prepared in manuscript.

Place	Date	Hour	Summary of Events and Information	Remarks and references to Appendices
	20th		10.5cm Howitzer fired a few rounds on T.17.a. "TART" and "TURK" active and punished. Working party seen in Trench N.36.B.10.30 and carrying parties on road 0.25.a, both dispersed by "A/153". Weather cold and misty. Visibility fair.	
	21st		"TURK" and "TART" active. At 11 am carrying parties were seen on road in O.25.a and were dispersed by "A/153". A shoot was carried out at request of Infantry 8 hits were obtained on dug out at 0.31.c. 45.10 by 4.5 Howitzers out of 25 rounds. Weather cold and misty. Visibility bad.	
	22nd		TURK and TART active and punished. Hostile artillery below normal. A working party of 6 men were seen digging at O.32.a 30.70 at 10.50 am and dispersed by B/153 during the day 3 hostile planes flew over T.4 and were engaged by our AA guns.	
	23rd	2 pm	A heavy T.M and artillery bombardment commenced at 2 pm and lasted till 6 pm to the right of the Divisional front, as a preliminary to a raid carried out by the Germans. Weather fine and cold. Visibility bad owing to mist. Artillery fairly active shelling T.17.a T.3. & T.3.6 with Howitzers, the latter place being shelled with lachrymatory shells. TART & TURK again active and punished. Many of the heavy T.M. bombs, which fell, being "duds". A enemy planes were up during the day but only one	

Army Form C. 2118.

WAR DIARY
INTELLIGENCE SUMMARY
(Erase heading not required.)

153rd Brigade
Royal Field Artillery

Title pages: JANUARY 1917

Place	Date	Hour	Summary of Events and Information	Remarks and references to Appendices
	23rd		one crossed the lines and came over Hill 63 flying in a S.W. direction. All three planes appeared to be acting in conjunction with Artillery. Weather fine and cold. Visibility fair; difficult to see at times.	
	24th		Hostile artillery active in morning on front line. T.M. "TART" was active in afternoon. During the day 6 different hostile planes crossed the lines, 2 of them flew over "A/153's" position in T.3. At 4.10 one of our planes, which had crossed the lines & was flying over MESSINES was attacked by 3 or 4 of our planes & forced to descend. It disappeared behind the ridge spiralling down. Weather cold & clear. At 11.25 pm a pre-arranged bombardment of the cross roads in MESSINES was carried out by the Divl and Heavy Artillery when the train from COMMINES arrived. A further bombardment was carried out half an hour afterwards. 1,000 rounds were fired altogether.	
	25.		Artillery much more active than usual. 7/1/72 Battery position at T.17 a 4032 fm shelled from 8-15 am to 12 noon by about 300 rounds 8"- 15 cm Hows. Two direct hits were obtained in No 3 pit & the gun was smashed & one was sustained by the telephone pit which however, was not damaged; shell dug-outs were damaged. No casualties were suffered. The position of the enemy battery was worked out as T.27 a 40 91. The magnetic bearing from the Target	

Army Form C. 2118.

WAR DIARY
or
INTELLIGENCE SUMMARY.
(Erase heading not required.)

153rd Brigade
Royal Field Artillery

JANUARY 1917

Place	Date	Hour	Summary of Events and Information	Remarks and references to Appendices
	26th		Target being 55° and the range as worked out by slip-wash and worked out as 5750 yards, this latter being 100 yards shorter than map range, probably due to the NE wind blowing at the time. All the fuzes found were of a new type altogether, bell-shaped, completely of brass, consisting of two parts, the top portion being a cap similar to that in DoPP Z 92, the markings being G.T. Z 92. During the shelling two hostile planes were observing most of the time & their signals were picked up by our wireless. Aeroplane generally active. Weather fine. Visibility good. Artillery very active with bombs. Nothing worth. From 8.15am 1pm B/153's position at T.16.2.6332 was heavily shelled by 300/400 rounds 15 cm How's, probably the same enemy battery as yesterday. One direct hit was obtained in No 3 pit through the opening & the gun was smashed. Another was sustained by a dug-out. The frame at T.16.d.25.75 received 3 direct hits much damage being done. 3 casualties were sustained, one very bad case, the limber gunner of No 3 who received 30 different wounds. The shooting was very accurate, the tracing being traversed most of the day. During part of the time the detached section of 60 pdrs in T.23.a was shelled also, result unknown. During the afternoon & evening occasional rounds were fired at "B/153". During the bombardment hostile planes were observing & their signals were picked up by our wireless	

Army Form C. 2118.

WAR DIARY or INTELLIGENCE SUMMARY
(Erase heading not required.)

153rd Brigade Royal Field Artillery

JANUARY 1917

Place	Date	Hour	Summary of Events and Information	Remarks and references to Appendices
	27th		wireless. Our counter-battery and aeroplane work were practically Nil. Another of our planes was forced down at 4-10 pm behind MESSINES in flames, the pilot making a good landing. Extreme frost in morning. Weather fine & cold. Visibility good. Aerial activity on the part of the enemy was very great all day. 2 planes came over T.3 at 10-45 am & circled round over T.10, 11, 16 & 17. till 11-15 am when they dropped some smoke signals & flew off in the direction of LA BASSEVILLE. They were thought to be of the "Albatross type". Our A.A. guns did very bad shooting & none of our planes endeavoured to engage them. 2 planes flew over T.18. at 3-45 pm but returned in a few minutes towards MESSINES. Weather fine & very frosty. Visibility fair.	
	28th		"TURK" & "TART" active & punished severely. A new trench is being dug from M.2.c.96.80 to M.2.d.25.80. Fresh posts for wire have been erected at O.32.c.35.85. A hostile plane crossed our lines over M.8 but were driven back by our A.A. guns. Weather fine & very frosty. Visibility good. Artillery fairly active. A direct hit was obtained on the hostile battery to the heavy T.M. position at N.36.c.48.20 causing considerable damage. O.33 & the road near BUS FARM was shelled persistently yesterday evening & early this morning. At 10-15 am 2 hostile planes flew over	
	29th			

Army Form C. 2118.

WAR DIARY or INTELLIGENCE SUMMARY

(Erase heading not required.)

153rd Brigade Royal Field Artillery

Place	Date	Hour	Summary of Events and Information	Remarks and references to Appendices
	29th		over U.1.d. A hostile plane flew over "A/153" position between 11·35 am & 12 noon. They were badly fired at by our AA guns & of our planes, 3 in number, which were up, only one endeavoured to chase them & it got engaged by hostile AA guns near the lines. Weather fine & frosty. Visibility fair.	
	30th		Artillery fairly active. The enemy carried out a concentrated bombardment between 12·5 pm and 12·10 pm on trenches U.1.a. - T.6.z. probably on a working party of ours there. About 60-60 77 & 105 m.m. shells were fired. "TURK" and "TART" were active in afternoon & were severely dealt with. 2 Germans were seen to leave BELL FARM at 10·30 am. Weather fine & frosty. Visibility good.	
	31st		A 105 m/m counter battery was very active from 1·30 - 5·30 pm on the Howitzer Batteries in T.18.c. about 90 rounds were fired. 3 casualties were suffered by one of the batteries, a sergeant being killed. The direction of the battery was taken from O.P.T.12.a & was found to be 42° True bearing which places the battery at O.35.d.4.25.2 probably. "TART" & "TURK" were again active at 11-15 am firing 80 rounds on trenches N.36.c.3-8 & were severely punished. A hostile plane was up most of the afternoon registering for the counter battery, hovering over the lines. It was not engaged by either of our planes or our AA guns. 2 balloons were up on bearings of 160° & 120° mag. respectively from T.16.d.60.39. One was seen to descend 4·20 pm. Two German aircraft were seen during the morning on different places between 7·35 & 8·10 am & were wiring at 0·31.a.90·15" between 7·35 & 8·10 am & 4 also were seen during the morning on different places. Weather cold - visibility fair.	

JANUARY 31st 1917.

M C O'Hara. Major. R.F.A.
Commanding 153rd Brigade R.F.A.

Army Form C. 2118.

WAR DIARY
or
INTELLIGENCE SUMMARY.
(Erase heading not required.)

153rd BRIGADE
Royal Field Artillery.

Vol/4

FEBRUARY 1917

Place	Date	Hour	Summary of Events and Information	Remarks and references to Appendices
MAP 1-20,000 28.S.W. ROEGSTEERT T21d12010	1-2-17		Hostile Counter Batteries were active on the positions of D/153 and D/173 in the late afternoon of to-day. They did little damage receiving two direct hits on D/173c position — in all about 200 shells were fired. T.M's were active during the early bombardment in our sector, the majority of the activity taking place on our left. Men were seen at various points in the German lines. SLOPING ROOF and UPPER HELL FARMS, also at O.25 Central. At 5-15 am the sector on our left was heavily bombarded by hostile artillery. "S.O.S" signals came over Hill 63 apparently observing the effect of the shooting on D/153. Enemy planes came over our fire was feeble and bad. Our planes were not visible, and A.A guns	
	2nd		Hostile artillery was very quiet. Hostile planes crossed our lines at 10.40 am + 1 pm, without hindrance from our planes. A.A gun fire very bad. Hostile planes crossed and re-crossed our lines throughout the day as they liked.	
	3rd		Hostile artillery was much quieter than it has been for some time. Last of the trees in front of KRUISTRAAT CABARET cut down. Hostile planes crossed and recrossed our lines without much opposition. Enemy aircraft have never been so active for some time.	
	4"		At about 4 + 5am a hostile patrol of 5 was seen in front T6.C + was fired on by out Lewis guns	

WAR DIARY
INTELLIGENCE SUMMARY

153rd BRIGADE Royal Field Artillery

February 1917

Date	Hour	Summary of Events and Information	Remarks and references to Appendices
4th		guns and rifles. Daylight disturbed 2 dead germans. At 10.45am a large notice was put up in enemy's lines "LET SAVE TWO WOUNDED CAMERADS ANSWER" (sic) Several periscopes appeared near by. At 11-30 am about 12 germans (3 of whom were officers) were looking over at this point & about 25 were looking over in another part of the line. We airpellid and then shouted that 2 men would come out & bring the bodies to our wire. Several immediately came out headed by a subaltern of about 18 years & 5 walked through wire, 2 carrying on prisoner up the body and towing it back to their lines. They then made signals to fetch the other but we forbade them. They went in and took down the board. 1 German only (by command) wore steel helmet. None wore gas masks, arms or equipment. Some wore strideni braun wearing a white brassard with red cross. One man wore the Iron Cross. The enemy troops were SAXON.	
5th		Artillery very quiet during the day. In the evening Hostile Machineguns were very active notes "TART" & "TURK" were active but were immediately punished by our artillery and Trench Mortars. Hostile aircraft were active flying over our lines when to where they would. "B" & "D" Batteries took part in the bombardment on the left Division front.	
6th		Hostile artillery normal. Trench Mortars were quite silent throughout the day. A certain amount of movement was seen at & round O.25.d.45.62 & N.31.d.95.48. Aeroplanes were fairly active. A short	

Army Form C. 2118.

WAR DIARY
of
INTELLIGENCE SUMMARY.
(Erase heading not required.)

February 1917

153rd Brigade Royal Field Artillery

Place	Date	Hour	Summary of Events and Information	Remarks and references to Appendices
	6th		Shoot was carried out in conjunction with 13th R.I.R. on U.2.a.30.15 - good results were obtained.	
	7th		Hostile artillery & mortars were very quiet. A considerable amount of new work appears to be going on at U.2.b.12.95 & U.2.d.40.60. Hostile planes were very active. A drum has been made from the enemy front line into "NO MANS LAND" at U.2.c.82.96.	
	8th		Hostile planes were reconnoitring active crossing our lines & on few occasions penetrating as far as BAILLEUL. Remainder of day quiet.	
	9th		Hostile artillery was more active than during the last few days. "TART & TURK" were active on the left of our zone. Considerable movement was seen at 4 HUNS FARM which was shelled by A/153. Aircraft activity still very active. D/153 took part in Bombardment on our right. Weather cold and misty.	
	10th		Between 8 & 10 AM about 200-150 m/m shells fell in T.11.a T.10.6. 10/153's position was mysteries by aeroplane in the afternoon. About 12 105 m/m shells were fired in all. The place was over the position for 2 hours. At 4 pm the farm at T.36.44.80 and neighbourhood shelled by 105's & 77 m/m shells. Major GALE & Lieut. BROWNING (both A/153) being slightly wounded. At 11.10 AM much more channel sound at Rhine FARM – R.enemy is apparently in process of ?	

Army Form C. 2118.

WAR DIARY
INTELLIGENCE SUMMARY.
(Erase heading not required.)

153rd Brigade
Royal Field Artillery

February 1917

Place	Date	Hour	Summary of Events and Information	Remarks and references to Appendices
	10th		and was fired at by A/153. Hostile planes were active & a bomb was dropped nr. ALDERSHOT CAMP at 2pm. Weather cold and frosty. Visibility good	
	11th		TURK & TART active in morning and afternoon. A working party was reported at N.36.d.60.30 by the infantry and was fired at by A/153 at 4.10 pm. Another was observed by C/153 at 0.25 & 20.23 and fired at. Several hostile planes flew over our lines. Visibility good	
	12th		TART & TURK active. Visibility almost impossible owing to mist	
	13th		TURK & TART active & punished by A & D Batteries. Weather fine but cloudy. Hostile artillery inactive. Visibility fair in afternoon.	
	14th	12.55 AM	A hurricane bombardment of 105 m/m & T.Ms. was opened on the trenches in M.I. It lifted at about 1.20 am. A raiding party entered, remained in the trenches for about 5 minutes & took about 3 of our men, one of whom was recovered, shot dead in our wire the next day. The raiders left behind 2 bags of grenades, a rough wooden box & explosive with detonator & fuze which was charged on if it had been left but failed to burn. A coat and cap. The latter with chevron arabic were recovered. Our casualties were 1 officer & 5 O.R. killed, 9 O/R wounded & 2 missing. A "S.O.S" was sent up but was not seen, but "Batteries fired on SOS" lines at 1.5 am, a message being received from the R.F. Bay by telephone. All was quiet by 1.40 am	Artillery

WAR DIARY of INTELLIGENCE SUMMARY

Place: 153rd Brigade Royal Field Artillery
Date: February 1917

Date	Hour	Summary of Events and Information
14th		Artillery & T.Ms slightly active on ft. System. In evening T.17 & T.23 were shelled with 105 & 150 m/m. A party of about 25 men were seen at 9.55 am at O.32.a.0290 laying a wooden tramway from O.32.a.0290 laying a wooden tramway from O.32.a.10.83 - O.31.b.9070. Material being brought down on a trolley which came into view at 4 Houses Farm. The party were dispersed by G & D Batteries. 4 men observed pushing the trolley back to the Farm. Single members of the party were seen at
	10 am	A new stretch of wooden posts without wire is being erected between O.32.a.45.11 - 45.02.
		6 Hostile planes were over during the day. 3 of them flying low behind HILL 63.
	6.30 pm	On sighting a party of the enemy about 20 strong near we were at 11.10 & suspecting a silent raid, the SOS signal was put up & our artillery barraged our front till 7.45 pm. Enemy retaliation strong for a short period & we suffered 8 casualties.
		Mist lifted at 9.30 am after which visibility was good.
15th		Artillery normal. At 2.45 pm & 105 m/m burst high over North of NEUVE EGLISE. T.M. machine. New heavy stam can be seen along hedge at O.31.d.1050-3050. 5 hostile planes were over, mostly T.T. One of them appeared over RORTEPYP at 4.50 pm flying very low from direction of BAILLEUL. It managed to clear the trees along the NEUVE EGLISE - DE SEULE Road and when over NEUVE EGLISE was engaged by AA guns, when he began to climb and turned westwards, On nearing his own

WAR DIARY
INTELLIGENCE SUMMARY

February 1917

153rd Brigade Royal Field Artillery

Place	Date	Hour	Summary of Events and Information	Remarks and references to Appendices
	15th		Winds and rain. Under a heavy rifle and M. Gun fire he seemed to lose control turned and came down in U.19.f. The pilot, who was only slightly wounded was captured. The enemy blew a mine at U.1.f.6050, a very bad explosion was heard & no flash was seen. A dense cloud of smoke & dust & much debris fell in our trench. Nissen huts cold clear. Visibility good. Artillery quiet. Enemy fired between 10 & 11pm about 10 rounds of 105 m/m. HE round T.9.d. 10b0. TMs inactive. It is thought that TURK & TART were moved down south to fire during enemy raid on 11.10 on the 14th & had not been moved back as yet. 2 hostile planes were up, one came over HILL 63. Weather fine but misty. Visibility good.	
	16th		Artillery quiet, except for retaliation promised by the raid carried out by 25 Division. 1355 A.438 AK & 2443. Bx were fired in support of this raid which took place at 10.41 am after 1 minutes bombt on the enemy's trenches round FACTORY FARM & neighbourhood. 2 germans were captured & many killed & several dugouts were bombed. Weather fine & misty, began to rain in morning. Visibility difficult.	
	17th		Between 8 & 8.45 am trenches M.1.4, 5, & 6 were heavily shelled by 105 m/m shells. At 3.45 pm T6.4 - N36.9. were shelled with 50 M/m shells. TAPE was silent & punished 3 times. This TM has not been active for 5 weeks & is probably on alternative position for TART or TURK who have formed their positions	
	18th			

Army Form C. 2118.

WAR DIARY
INTELLIGENCE SUMMARY.
(Erase heading not required.)

February 1917

153rd Brigade
Royal Field Artillery

Place	Date	Hour	Summary of Events and Information	Remarks and references to Appendices
	18th		positions untenable. In the same way "TOR" was nature for the first time for 5 weeks. At 1.35 pm Enemy sent up 50 Very Lights between SWAYNES FARM and MESSINES (observed from N.36.2.) with no result except a slight shelling round N.MIDLAND FARM which seems nearly every day. At 4.6 pm 12 rockets were sent up from enemy line south of SNIPER'S HOUSE; these appeared to burst into showers of golden rain at their summit - there was no apparent result. Weather showery & very windy. Visibility bad. A distinct earth tremor was felt at 6.45 pm	
	19th		A daylight raid was carried out by the 16th Div at 7.15 am. Our artillery gave assistance and 1800 rounds bombarding as soon as the barrel took place. The raid was unsuccessful. The enemy appeared to be quite prepared and it lacked surprise. Enemy machine guns opened fire at once, the party operating on our left was met by bombs and rifle grenades and was forced to return before they reached the enemy's wire. The centre party was met by T.M. Bombs. The raiders received several casualties and sent infantry, who co-operated with smoke bombs and machine guns, had 4 including 1 Officer wounded. Enemy retaliation was not very great. DURHAM ROAD and AGNES St being bombarded with 77 and 105 m/m Shells during the day. Weather fine but very windy. Visibility bad. It is reported that another earth tremor was felt at 5.10 am.	

… Army Form C. 2118.

WAR DIARY
INTELLIGENCE SUMMARY
(Erase heading not required.)

February 1917

153rd Brigade Royal Field Artillery

Place	Date	Hour	Summary of Events and Information	Remarks and references to Appendices
	20th		A T.M Bombardment was carried out from 1.30 – 1.50 pm on the trenches round MORTAR FARM including the support, reserve and C.T.s. Much material damage was caused. 2 T.Ms fired 130 bombs, STOKES MORTARS 1600 rounds. 6" Howitzers fired 80 rounds and the GROUP fired 1200 rounds. Machine guns also fired and counter batteries should be. The retaliation provoked was very small. 40. 77 m/m and 20 105 m/m shells falling in N.36.c. 10-15 rounds of 105 m/m were fired at front line in N.1.c. & N. MIDLAND FARM. This latter is probably a calibration point as enemy fires a few rounds at it every day. N.13 also received some 150 mm shells. Weather wet and misty. Visibility bad.	
	21st		Artillery machine with exception of a small bombardment with 77 m/m shells about 40 in all on T.6.b. A group retaliation was fired (VGL4.) & the hostile artillery ceased. Weather fine but misty. Visibility bad.	
	22nd		At 5-45 am this morning a bombardment was heard on the right. All was quiet on our front. The enemy carried out a raid to right of our Division in which 5 of our men were killed & one of his men left behind dead. Weather fine but misty. Visibility Nil.	
	23rd		Hostile artillery machine except for 20. 77m/m shells fired at N.36.c. at 2.15 pm. A raid was carried out by the Div. on our left, to which we gave artillery support, firing about 700 rounds.	

Army Form C. 2118.

WAR DIARY
INTELLIGENCE SUMMARY
(Erase heading not required.)

February 1917

153rd Brigade.
Royal Field Artillery

Place	Date	Hour	Summary of Events and Information	Remarks and references to Appendices
	23rd		rounds in all. The raid was a failure, the Germans being on the alert with bombs and machine guns and the enemy's trenches were not entered. Weather misty. Visibility nil.	
	24th		Front work & visible in UGLY TRENCH. A working party was seen here at 3-6 pm and dispersed by A/153. Weather fine but misty. Visibility poor.	
	25th		About 8 77mm shells fell in N.36.c. the WULVERGHEM-MESSINES Road was shelled and over 200 Lachrymatory shells were put in T.17. G/A.K. were repaired by the Liaison Officer in firing at suspected snipers posts along the STEENEBEEK. Weather fine & misty. Visibility bad.	
	26th		Hostile artillery much more active than usual. 60 x 105mm fell near BONES FARM in morning, 45 rounds 77 + 105 mm fell near IRISH FARM, 35 rounds 77 + 105mm fell near U.7.a in afternoon. New wire is visible at 50 yards each side of U.2.a.14.96. About 80 concrete blocks are lying on parapet & parados at U.2.a.14.96. Pile of timber is visible at U.2a 1882. Trench along hedge O.31.d 46.65 - 40.61 is under repair. At 12 noon a working party of 12 was seen at O.1.9.d 40.10 & dispersed by B/153. Weather fine. Visibility good.	
	27th		Hostile artillery and T.M. machine Weather fine but misty. Visibility poor.	

Army Form C. 2118.

153rd Brigade
Royal Field Artillery

WAR DIARY
or
INTELLIGENCE SUMMARY.
(Erase heading not required.)

February 1917

Place	Date	Hour	Summary of Events and Information	Remarks and references to Appendices
	28th		a. T.M was active (probably TART) at 8.30 am firing 12 rounds in N.36.b.r.3 and was punished. 7 - 77mm shells were fired into N.35.d. otherwise hostile artillery was very quiet all day. At 9.20 am a working party was heard by the Infantry at BIRTHDAY FARM and reported to "B"/153 who fired at the farm. Owing to the mist the result was unknown. At 11-15 am another working party was seen at N.36.d. 60.70 & dispersed by A/153. Weather fine but misty. Visibility poor.	

February 28th 1917

W.C. Thomson
Lt. Col. R.F.A.
Command 153rd Brigade R.F.A

Army Form C. 2118.

153rd Brigade. Royal Field Artillery

WAR DIARY
or
INTELLIGENCE SUMMARY
(Erase heading not required.)

MARCH 1917.

Wt 15

Place	Date 1917	Hour	Summary of Events and Information	Remarks and references to Appendices
MAP. 1-20,000 28. S.W. PLOEGSTEERT T.21.d. 20.10.	MARCH 1st		Enemy artillery very active owing to clear fine weather. "C" + "B" Batteries were registered by balloon + aeroplane & "B" Batty was shelled with about 700 shells of 15 cm How. It is thought that some larger shells were used. The Battery position was badly damaged, 2 guns being smashed, all ammo. posts being removed & 3 casualties being sustained. Sound bearings were taken & it is believed that the hostile Batteries are in O.3.4.b. N MIDLAND FARM & trenches in U.1.a & T.6.b. were shelled with about 60, 105 & 150 m/m shells during the morning. In the evening a 10 cm Field Gun opened on the position with shrapnel. Pieces of the shells & fuzes were found. These belonged to 10 cm. Schr. 96. "TAPE" fired 3 rounds into N.36.b.2 & was severely punished. A concrete emplacement is visible at O.3.c. 20.80. Fresh work & new dugouts visible at N.30.d. 50.05. 2 strong dugouts are visible at O.3.c. 20.80. Fresh work & new dugouts visible at SCOTT FARM. A party of 50 Germans were seen at RAB POINT for a very short time. Party of 7 Germans unequipped & empty handed were seen on road at N.36.b.& 5.92. Hostile planes very active. Hostile balloons were up at the following true bearings between 11.45 am + 4 pm - 71° 39°. 51° 60° from O.P.T.12.a. Weather fine. Visibility very high.	
	2nd		150 m/m German batteries active on battery positions in T.16.d. T.17.a. c. throughout the day. Indications of shells being employed part of the time. 9. T.M. bombs fell in Trenches T6.5.a.b. but it is not known which T.M. fired them. There was very little retaliation for our night firing which was	

Army Form C. 2118.

WAR DIARY
INTELLIGENCE SUMMARY
(Erase heading not required.)

Place: 152nd Brigade Royal Field Artillery
Month: March 1917

Date	Hour	Summary of Events and Information	Remarks and references to Appendices
2nd		M.G. was carried out from 7pm 1-3-17 to 6 AM 2.3.17. There is a suspected dump at O.25.d.70.20 & a M.G emplacement at O.32.a.20.20. Weather fine but hazy.	
3rd		Hostile T.Ms & enemy machine. Snowing during morning. Very misty in afternoon. Observation almost impossible.	
4th		77 m/m guns active. 30 rounds on W.1.5.&.6. & 50 rounds at THATCHED COTTAGE which was set on fire. 10 - 105 m/m shells fell near B/152's position. Enemy working parties at N.36.d.16.02 & N.30.Z.70.00. was dispersed. A telescope was seen flashing from tower of L'INSTITUTION ROYALE at MESSINES at 1pm. It is thought that this was the O.P. for the battery shelling THATCHED COTTAGE. Planes over HILL 63, our battery position in T.16 & T.17 & 2 over A/152's position. Weather fine but hazy. Visibility fair.	
5th		Artillery & T.Ms inactive. Weather fine but very misty. Observation impossible.	
6th		"TINA" & "TURK" slightly active. Artillery normal. A few rounds 105 m/m fell in WULVERGHEM. We carried out a bombardment on the OISTER TRENCHES, the heavy artillery co-operating but owing to the fog it was very difficult to observe the effect. The retaliation was very feeble & ceased when we fired a Group Retaliation. During a lift in the mist at about 11am a man was seen repairing the roof of L'INSTITUTION ROYALE. 3 planes crossed the line, 2 of them flying over T.M. Weather fine but foggy. Visibility bad.	

Army Form C. 2118.

WAR DIARY / INTELLIGENCE SUMMARY

153rd Brigade. Royal Field Artillery

March 1917

Place	Date	Hour	Summary of Events and Information	Remarks and references to Appendices
	7th		Hostile artillery below normal. T.Ms very active. "TAPE" was active also "TINA" & "TURNIP"(N.36.d.75.37) — the latter fired 10 rounds on AGNES — DAY STREETS causing 3 casualties. "C153" was registered by plane with 20 rounds 105 m/m. We co-operated with RIGHT GROUP in a bombardment on OYSTER TRENCHES in which six 6", two 9.2" How'rs and 6 60 pdrs took part. The object was to simulate a raid with a creeping barrage & to destroy dugouts in the enemy's trenches. There was practically no retaliation. Weather fine but very windy. Visibility poor.	
	8th		At 3.30 p.m. the enemy opened a very heavy bombardment with T.M. Bombs, Wurfgranaten 77, 105" & 150 m/m shells & m.g's on our left sector & along the 16th Divl. front in connection with 5 daylight raids on the latter's front. We established & then at request of Rt. GROUP "16" Divn switched on to their front. Our casualties were very small, but our trenches were very badly damaged. 2 of the raiding parties only entered the 16th trenches & reaching the support line made away with over 30 prisoners leaving 10 killed & wounded in our lines. During the night enemy kept up intermittent M.G. & T.M. fire to prevent damage being repaired. Night firing was carried out from 7pm 8/3/17 to 6 am 9-3-17 by R. and Left Groups & Heavy artillery on 21.2 - 21.8. Weather cold with occasional snowstorms. Visibility very bad.	
	9th		At 4-7 a.m. a hurricane bombardment of T.Ms & field guns. It was opened on our left sector which	

Army Form C. 2118.

March 1917

WAR DIARY
or
INTELLIGENCE SUMMARY.
(Erase heading not required.)

153rd Brigade. Royal Field Artillery

Place	Date	Hour	Summary of Events and Information	Remarks and references to Appendices
	9th		which lifted over to our support lines. A raiding party endeavoured to enter the front line at N.36.a. 40.80 (16" Div) but were repulsed, with 2 prisoners & at least 6 dead inside our wire. Movement was noticed in enemy front line opposite our left subsector, but no nothing came of it. It is supposed that they were dummies. We opened a slow rate of fire on enemy's front line & then at request of RT G Roup. 16" Div's switched on to their front. All was quiet at 4.50 am. T.17.a. was shelled with 200 105 m/m shells in morning. A working party was observed at 0.19.d.80.75 which was shelled by 'G/153'. 16" Div were dropped on twice during the morning. One of them flew low over NEUVE EGLISE, passed over the 60 pdr Battery in T.15.d which was firing at the time & came down in U.9.c. probably attacked by our AA guns. Weather cold with snowstorms. Visibility bad.	
	10th		Artillery & T.M. very quiet except in morning. At 8.15 pm & 9pm about 30-40 rounds 150 m/m How. fell near SHANKHILL HUTS causing 7 casualties. The greater proportion were probably defected shells. Weather fine but very muddy. Visibility bad.	
	11th		Artillery very active. At 12.30 pm 50 rounds 105 m/m fell in T.17.a. 'B/153's position was shelled between 3.15 & 4 pm with 200/300 shells 15cm Howrs. or possibly 21cm. (judging by none	

T2134. Wt. W708—776. 500000. 4/15. Sir J. C. & S.

Army Form C. 2118.

WAR DIARY
or
INTELLIGENCE SUMMARY.
(Erase heading not required.)

153rd Brigade Royal Field Artillery

March 1917

Place	Date	Hour	Summary of Events and Information	Remarks and references to Appendices
	11th		normal. 9.3.g. of bursts and craters made.) 1 direct hit was obtained on a dugout causing 2 very bad concussions – 2 men being buried and 2 guns were damaged. Shelling recommenced at 5.30 pm stopping at 6 pm causing one other casualty – 20 rounds 150 m/m shell in all. 30. 77 m/m shells fell in T.15 b & d. at 3.15 pm. Between 4.15 pm & 6.15 pm SHANKHILL HUTS were intermittently shelled by 105 m/m shells & lethal shells, about 40 falling in aft. The Huns were firing from the direction of W/O Control (front observed from T.15 d 10.30) Several hostile planes were over our lines & at 1 pm 2 planes appeared out of a cloud & while one hovered above our balloon at NIEPPE, the other circled round it firing its machine gun into it. This it continued to do in spite of the fact that our AA guns were putting up a very heavy barrage, till the balloon descended in flames – the observer had already parachuted down.	
			Weather fine. Visibility fair. Enemy artillery normal. At 12.30 pm about 12 105 m/m shells fell near SHANKILL HUTS and	
	12th		shells fell near the PIGGERIES and PLOEGSTEERT. The first round near the PIGGERIES gave a brick red smoke in place of the normal flash. A/153's position received 50 105 m/m shells and an Infantry Officer was wounded by a shell entering the mess. T.18 received a few 77 & 105 m/m shells at 1.45 pm. A working party was seen behind the hedge at 0.31 6. 85 65 and was.	

WAR DIARY of 153rd Brigade Royal Field Artillery

March 1917

Army Form C. 2118.

Place	Date	Hour	Summary of Events and Information	Remarks and references to Appendices
	12th		was dispersed by D/153. At 2.50 p.m. a man was observed putting up telephone poles at 026c.2020 and was fired at by 6/153. Weather showery. Visibility poor.	
	13th		Enemy artillery quiet. The battery in T.17.b. was shelled with 90. 15 cm howitzer shells from 11-12 a.m. and 20 77 m/m shells fell near O.P. T.12.a. at 5.5 p.m. Weather fine. Visibility poor owing to mist.	
	14th		Enemy artillery and T.M's inactive. A few 77 m/m fell near 7.18.b. 75.90. from direction A.0.2.0.a. At 2.10 p.m. 30. 105 m/m shells fell on T.16.a.7. There was intermittent shelling of the NEUVE EGLISE - WULVERGHEM Road near NEUVE EGLISE. The farm buildings in T.16.c. were shelled with 50. 150 m/m Trench shells at 4.20 p.m. Weather fine. Visibility poor owing to mist.	
	15th		Enemy artillery normal. The 60 Pdr Battery in T.15.d. was registered with 150 m/m How" about 20 shells being burst high in the air. 25 77 m/m shells fell near LA GRANDE MUNQUE FARM at 12.20 p.m. and at same time 30. 105 m/m shells fell in T.18. At 3 p.m. a hostile plane flew over in the direction of NIEPPE apparently making for our billows there but was forced to return by our A.A. gun fire. Weather fine. Visibility fair.	
	16th		Hostile artillery normal. 2 working parties were observed at 025.d 9170 and 032.f 2025 and were	

Army Form C. 2118.

WAR DIARY
INTELLIGENCE SUMMARY.
(Erase heading not required.)

153rd Brigade Royal Field Artillery

March 1917

Place	Date	Hour	Summary of Events and Information	Remarks and references to Appendices
	16th		were dispersed by our fire. Enemy plane attempted to cross our lines N.E. of MESSINES but was driven off by our AA guns. Weather fine and sunny. Visibility poor owing to mist.	
	17th		The New Zealand Divisional Arty took over our Battery positions & Brigade HQ billets	
	18th		Brigade HQ marched to DRANOUTRE (M.35.d.90.40) this morning, the remainder of the Brigade taking up wagon Line positions in the neighbourhood of DRANOUTRE. The Brigade came out of action for the purpose of a rest.	
	19th		The Brigade still at DRANOUTRE	
	20th		— do —	
	21st		The Brigade marched to WAARBECQUES en route to LUMBRES	
	22nd		The Brigade after stopping the night at WAARBECQUES continued their march to LUMBRES arriving there in the afternoon complete	
	23rd & 24th		The Brigade commenced its training	
	25th		Divine Service held in the CHATEAU DE RAISME, LUMBRES (where Brigade H.Q. are) in the morning. The afternoon was considered as half-holiday.	
	26th		The Brigade continued training	
	27th		— do —	

Army Form C. 2118.

WAR DIARY
INTELLIGENCE SUMMARY.
(Erase heading not required.)

153rd Brigade Royal Field Artillery.

Place	Date	Hour	Summary of Events and Information	Remarks and references to Appendices
	28		Inspection of the whole Brigade by Brig. Genl. H.T. BROCK. RA.	
	29		Training continued	
	30		" "	
	31		The Army Commander & the MGRA inspected the Brigade this morning. Half holiday in the afternoon	

31st March 1917.

W. Thom__
Lt: Col RFA
Commanding 153rd Brigade RFA

Army Form C. 2118.

WAR DIARY
or
INTELLIGENCE SUMMARY.
(Erase heading not required.)

153rd Brigade Royal Field Artillery

Vol /5

Place	Date	Hour	Summary of Events and Information	Remarks and references to Appendices
LUMBRES	1-4-17		Sunday Divine Service held in the morning in the CHATEAU DE RAISME LUMBRES. (Brigade Headquarters)	
	2nd		Half holiday in the afternoon	
	3rd		The Brigade continued its training	
	4th		—do—	
	5th		—do—	
			The Brigade commenced the return journey to DRANOUTRE and stopped at WARDRECQUES for the night 5th/6th inst	
	6th		March continued. Brigade arrived at DRANOUTRE complete by 4 pm (HQ M.35.d.4.2.)	
	7th 8th 9th		Sections of "C" & "D" Batteries 153rd Brigade R.F.A. went into action during the nights 7/8th and 8th/9th instants	
	10th to 19th		Owing to the front of the Division being covered by one Brigade only namely:— 193rd Brigade R.F.A. the Batteries of two Brigades were put under the tactical command of 193rd Brigade R.F.A. Some sections of the Batteries have been put in action, others in action at rest	
	April 1917 (inc)			

Army Form C. 2118.

WAR DIARY
or
INTELLIGENCE SUMMARY.
(Erase heading not required.)

Place: 153rd Brigade Royal Field Artillery
April 1917

Date	Hour	Summary of Events and Information	Remarks and references to Appendices
20th to 21st		Acting on information obtained from a deserter of the 4th GRENADIER REGIMENT, 2nd Division which is opposite to our 40th Division night firing was carried out during the night 20th/21st inst from 8.30 pm to 5.30 am. The prisoner stated that a relief of his Regiment would be taking place during that night.	
22nd		In the afternoon our observation balloon in M.23.a was fired at by 2-10 cm guns which were brought up specially for that purpose and was punctured by fragments of shell. It commenced to descend & the 2 occupants (Officers) parachuted down to the ground safely. The balloon was brought in without much harm and when a ½ an hour was again in the air with the 2 observers.	
23rd		The observation balloon in S.11 was also fired at without effect later in the evening.	
24th to 25th		A few more rounds were fired at the balloon in S.11 this morning — no result. "A" and "B" 163 Batteries R.F.A. were placed in action at rest during the night.	
26th to 30th		Nothing to report	

Maj Colson
Major R.F.A.
Commandg 153rd Brigade R.F.A.

Army Form C. 2118.

WAR DIARY
or
INTELLIGENCE SUMMARY.
(Erase heading not required.)

153rd Brigade, Royal Field Artillery

May 1917.

Place	Date	Hour	Summary of Events and Information	Remarks and references to Appendices
DRANOUTRE M.35.d.40.20	1st		At 12 noon, acting on information gleaned from a prisoner, a daylight raid was carried out on SPANBROEK MOLEN. There was no bombardment, but a little desultory fire was carried out with the object of keeping the enemy's heads down. The party reached the enemy front line but at a point 150 yards South of the point arranged and found it unoccupied. Fire was opened on them from the support lines & from the point they should have gone to, and the party returned intact - the officer being slightly wounded. 15 to 20 Germans were counted in the front line and a machine gun was put on the parapet but was knocked out by our Lewis guns. No enemy retaliation or barrage was suffered.	
	2nd to 6th (inc)		Nothing to report.	
	7th		From 6.45 - 8.50 pm enemy guns and howitzer (except 12") in 2nd Army fired in retaliation for enemy firing on back area.	
	8th		Nothing of importance happened.	
	9th to 26th (inc)		Ammunition was brought up every evening by trams to the dumps at rear of KEMMEL HILL	

Army Form C. 2118.

WAR DIARY
INTELLIGENCE SUMMARY

153rd Brigade. Royal Field Artillery

May

(Erase heading not required.)

Instructions regarding War Diaries and Intelligence Summaries are contained in F. S. Regs., Part II. and the Staff Manual respectively. Title pages will be prepared in manuscript.

Place	Date	Hour	Summary of Events and Information	Remarks and references to Appendices
	27th		HILL and distributed to batteries an an average of 1300 rounds per gun.	
			From 10-12 pm ULSTER CAMP and the Wagon Lines between it and DRANOUTRE were heavily shelled by 10 cm guns. 2 hits were scored on the former and the C.R.E. was killed. 6 horses were killed and 8 others severely wounded (all put to death in the morning) by one shell. Several camps were hit and a rough estimate of the damage done is 6 personnel and horses is 74 men, 98 horses (killed and wounded) CROIX DE POPERINGE was also shelled. A great number of these shells appeared to be "blinds" or with a long delay action.	
	28th		The shelling recommenced at 12 midnight and ceased at 1 am. ST JANS CAPPEL was shelled also In the evening it re-opened from 10-11 pm and the neighbourhood of CROIX DE POPERINGE was shelled. The position occupied by "16/153" was shelled in the morning - two elephants being killed.	
	29th		From 10 pm onwards the area EAST of DRANOUTRE was shelled with 10 cm gun shells. These were probably gas as everyone appeared to fail to explode.	
	30th		At 3 am shelling recommenced and a direct hit was scored on a house at the N.E corner of DRANOUTRE. the LOCRE Road received a spraying of 13 cm gun shrapnel. The SPANBROEK	

WAR DIARY

May 1917.

153rd Brigade Royal Field Artillery

Army Form C. 2118.

Place	Date	Hour	Summary of Events and Information	Remarks and references to Appendices
			SPANBROEK GROUP ceased to exist and the "RIGHT MAIN" and "LEFT MAIN" GROUPS came into being, the "RIGHT" being commanded by Lt.Col. SIMPSON DSO. RFA and the "LEFT" by Lt.Col. R.G. THOMSON DSO RFA (HQ DRANOUTRE) the "RIGHT" GROUP still continued to maintain the defence of the whole line. The "LEFT" GROUP now consists of the 153rd Brigade RFA the 86th Army Brigade (commanded by Lt.Col. F.C. BRYANT. C.M.G.) and the 108th Army Brigade (commanded by Lt.Col. W.H. DRAKE C.M.G.) and is divided into 2 sub-groups :- "C" and "D". "C" consisting of "A" "C" "D" 76. B/153. "C" + D 108 and "D" consisting of "A" "B"/108, "A" "C" + "D"/153 B/76. In the evening BAILLEUL-METEREN Road was shelled by a high velocity gun. About 20 shells in all fell	
	31st		From 2.30 am to 11am the cross roads at N.21 d 40.40 and at 3 am DRANOUTRE and West of it were shelled by 77 + 105 m/m + 10cm guns and 3 hits were scored on houses in the village. Wire cutting was carried out by "A" "B" "C" 153. Brigade and a small bombardment by Howitzers. At 9.10 pm one of our balloons in direction of STEENWERK which was being engaged by a 10 cm gun turst into flames + descended slowly to the ground. The occupants were seen to parachute down.	

Army Form C. 2118.

WAR DIARY

INTELLIGENCE SUMMARY. 153rd Brigade. Royal Field Artillery

(Erase heading not required.)

May 1917

Place	Date	Hour	Summary of Events and Information	Remarks and references to Appendices
	31st		At 10 pm a high velocity gun opened fire on the WEST of DRANOUTRE and BAILLEUL and continued up to 12 midnight - about 40 rounds were fired in all. One shell dropped in the road (DRANOUTRE - BAILLEUL) making a crater 6ft deep and 18ft across, others dropped in the fields around and one fell on a limber in the Wagon line of A/84 Bde destroying it and two other limbers. Only 2 casualties to horses and one to men were reported.	

May 31st 1917

R.V. Thomson
Lt. Col. R.F.A.
Commanding 153rd Brigade R.F.A.

WAR DIARY

INTELLIGENCE SUMMARY.
153rd. BRIGADE. ROYAL FIELD ARTILLERY.

JUNE. 1917.

Army Form C. 2118.

Place	Date	Hour	Summary of Events and Information	Remarks and references to Appendices
DRANOUTRE. M35d.40-20	1st		In the early morning a 13 cm. Naval HV gun fired WEST of DRANOUTRE. Several of the shells fell around the Wagon Lines doing some damage. One crater on the main DRANOUTRE-BAILLEUL Road was 6 ft deep and 18 ft across. Night firing was continued on enemy's trenches and approaches.	
	2nd		"U" DAY. The programme for this day was carried out according to 2nd Army Scheme. BAILLEUL Station was again shelled in early morning.	
	3rd		"V" DAY. A bombardment of WYTSCHAETE by artillery of all calibres was carried out at 11 a.m. lasting till 11-30 a.m. and was followed by a creeping smoke barrage along the Divisional front under cover of which PECKHAM was raided. A good fight was put up by enemy everywhere, but the raiders succeeded in bringing back 16 prisoners. The daily programme was also carried out.	
	4th		"W" DAY. A creeping smoke barrage was put down along the whole front and under cover of this SPANBROEK MOLEN was raided - 1 officer and 30 o/r were captured and about 20 o/r killed. The daily programme was carried out. This included wire cutting.	
	5th		"X" DAY. The daily programme was carried out as usual.	
	6th		"Y" DAY. The daily programme of bombardment was carried out according to plan. The 153rd. Brigade. RFA. Headquarters moved to REGENT ST DUG-OUTS (Battle HQ)N.29.c.45-45.	
	7th		"Z" DAY. The assault took place at 3-10 a.m. following the explosion of 3 mines under the German Front and Support Lines on our Divisional front. Very little opposition was met with excepting from isolated M.Gs and snipers. By 10 a.m. the WYTSCHAETE-MESSINES Ridge was in our hands including the villages themselves. A halt of 5 hours for consolidation was made on the BLACK LINE (E of the Ridge) while the wire in front of the OOSTAVERNE LINE was being cut by our artillery, and a protective barrage was kept in front of this line. At 3-10 p.m. a fresh advance took place and by 4 p.m. the final objective, the OOSTAVERNE LINE, was in our hands. The enemy made a few spasmodic and feeble counter attacks which were quickly broken up by our barrage. contd -	

Army Form C. 2118.

(2).

JUNE 1917. WAR DIARY INTELLIGENCE SUMMARY.

153rd. BRIGADE. ROYAL FIELD ARTILLERY.

(Erase heading not required.)

Instructions regarding War Diaries and Intelligence Summaries are contained in F.S. Regs., Part II. and the Staff Manual respectively. Title pages will be prepared in manuscript.

Place	Date	Hour	Summary of Events and Information	Remarks and references to Appendices
	8th		Our artillery put down several protective barrages and fired in response to various 'S.O.S' Calls. At 7 p.m. a feeble counter attack was launched by the enemy opposite MESSINES, but this object was not attained and we took several prisoners. The night was quiet.	
	9th		"A" & "D" Batteries.153rd.Bde.RFA. advanced to forward positions on the ridge in O.19.c. During night a programme of night firing was carried out. Enemy's artillery was very quiet all day.	
	10th		153.Bde.RFA.HQ., moved to IRISH HOUSE (N.23.c.85-75) from REGENT ST DUG-OUTS. "B" & "C" Batteries 153.Bde.RFA. advanced to positions in O.19.c. Hostile artillery active, firing on both sides of ridge. Hostile planes very active.	
	11th		Hostile artillery active, firing on both sides of ridge. Hostile planes very active.	
	12th		Enemy artillery less active. At 3 p.m. and 9 p.m 7 E.A. flew over ridge very low. They were engaged neither by our AA guns nor planes.	
	13th		In early morning 7 E.A. flew over our lines very low and harassed our infantry with machine gun fire. Enemy artillery very quiet with exception of a little desultory firing by artillery of various calibres near the 3 18-pdr batteries of this brigade.	
	14th		Enemy artillery fairly active. E.A. also active.	
	15th		At 10-30 p.m. the neighbourhood of KEMMEL was shelled by 20 rounds from a long range gun. Between 4 & 6-15 p.m. the enemy carried out a bombardment on our trenches in O.26.a. and O.32.d. A hostile battery was observed firing at a true bearing of 740 from O.27.a.O5-60. 7 E.A. again flew over the ridge and were not interfered with either by our AA guns or planes. A	

Army Form C. 2118.

WAR DIARY
INTELLIGENCE SUMMARY

153rd. BRIGADE. ROYAL FIELD ARTILLERY.

(Erase heading not required.)

Instructions regarding War Diaries and Intelligence Summaries are contained in F.S. Regs., Part II. and the Staff Manual respectively. Title pages will be prepared in manuscript.

JUNE 1917.

Place	Date	Hour	Summary of Events and Information	Remarks and references to Appendices
	16th		A covering barrage was put down in support of reconnoitring patrols sent out by our Infantry. Aggressive firing was kept up all day. Hostile artillery active firing all over the sector. Our front and support trenches were bombarded with 15 cm between 5-45 p.m. and 6 p.m. A 13 cm HV gun fired in squares N.24 and O.19. during the night. In the early morning KEMMEL was shelled with 5.9" or 4.2" gun causing casualties to personnel and horses in the wagon lines. Enemy aeroplanes were very active flying very low over our trenches in batches of 6. They were engaged by our AA guns, but not by our planes. 1 of our planes was brought down. An enemy balloon was visible from O.27.a.32-28 at 81O true bearing. 3 Germans were seen near O.24.c.30-60. In evening enemy artillery very active. O.19, 20 and 21 were shelled persistently between 8 and 9-30 p.m. by 150 m/m Hows and 13 cm HV gun. At 9-52 p.m. an "S.O.S" signal was sent up to which we replied. All was quiet by 10-30 p.m.	
	17th		Enemy artillery active. The ridge was intermittently shelled by 13 cm gun and 150 mm Howitzer between 4 and 8 am and with 105 mm between 8-30 and 9-10 am. E.A. active.	
	18th		Enemy artillery inactive. E.A. fairly active, flying over our lines.	
	19th		E. Artillery inactive, except usual firing on West side of ridge. During night WARNETON Line and approaches to it were kept under fire.	
	20th 21st		The Brigade was withdrawn to its wagon lines. Bde HQ. went in advance to the SCHAEKKEN area. The batteries of this brigade moved to the SCHAEKKEN area.	
	22nd - 26th		Rest and Training.	
	26th		Brigade moved back to Wagon Lines and 1 section from each battery relieved 1 section of 58th Bde R.F.A. batteries. HQ's wagon line was at N.19.b.27-37. In	

Army Form C. 2118.

WAR DIARY

INTELLIGENCE SUMMARY.   153rd.BRIGADE.RFA.,

(Erase heading not required.)

JUNE 1917.

Place	Date	Hour	Summary of Events and Information	Remarks and references to Appendices
	27th		In evening the rest of each battery went into action and HQ's moved to S.P.12 (N.23.b.23-30). At 8-15 p.m. about 50 rounds 105 mm gas shells fell in vicinity of N.23.a.50-60. 3 E.A. were over 0.19 at 9 p.m.	
	28th		E.artillery less active than usual. Between 3 & 4 a.m. about 60 150 mm shell were fired into 0.19.a. & c. and about 20 gas shells in vicinity of IRISH HOUSE. Between 1-30 and 1-45 pm about 30 rounds 150 mm shell fell round 0.19.c.44-54. Between 4-45 pm and 7 pm about 140 150 mm shell fell in N.30 b & d and 0.25.a. 3 E.A. were over 0.19. at 10 a.m. and single planes during the day, especially between 6 & 9 p.m. Between 4 & 8 pm 9 E.Balloons were observed from 0.29.c.56-29 at true bearings of 1400, 1230, 1160, 1130, 1040, 980, 740, 550 and 610.	
	29th		Hostile artillery inactive except in early morning - between midnight and 2 a.m. - when about 100 rounds 77 and 150 mm fell in 0.19.c. and at 11 a.m. when 30 105 mm shells fell in 0.19.a.& c. The same balloons as were reported yesterday were up at 3 p.m. At 1-20 p.m. E.A. were over our lines and at 1-45 p.m. one was brought down in 0.17. by our AA fire. During the evening they were also very active.	
	30th		Enemy artillery normal. "C/153's" position at 0.19.c.50-59 was shelled with about 80 rounds 150 mm. No damage was done and the counter battery was called on and engaged the hostile battery. Visibility bad owing to mist and rain.	

R.E. Thomson.
Lt-Col. R.F.A.
Commanding.153rd.Brigade.R.F.A.

30th June 1917.

Army Form C. 2118.

WAR DIARY
or
INTELLIGENCE SUMMARY.
(Erase heading not required.)

153rd Brigade R.F.A. October 1917.

Vol 22

Place	Date	Hour	Summary of Events and Information	Remarks and references to Appendices
METZ-EN-COUTURE	1/10/17		As the enemy has discovered and engaged all our battery positions with effect, night firing from our Howitzers is being carried out from single guns not from single guns at B.6.d.60.90. and B.9.c.80.17.	
	2/10/17		American Naval Officer visited the Battery positions. T.M. shoot given for two Stokes Mortar right firing from single guns.	
	3/10/17		B. Battery commenced firing 6 Battery single gun shoot. Last two in 27/Div. normal at enemy horse lines firing at A.15.33.	
	4/10/17		Round not of day. Corps Commander visited Wagon Lines. Usual night firing.	
	5/10/17		Enemy engaged on A.15.33 at night gun with 5.9s Howitzer battery was asked for, of 500 rounds fired in all during the day and a gun emplacement destroyed. Two projectors were fired from R.26.c at 10.30 PM. Right group formed enemy fire.	
	6/10/17		Owing to bad visibility hostile artillery was quiet. The 12th R.I.R. carried out a violent raid on WIGAN COPSE at 10·0 PM and after encountering	

WAR DIARY
INTELLIGENCE SUMMARY
(Erase heading not required.)

Army Form C. 2118.

Place: Wither (?)   153rd Brigade 1/7/17

Date	Hour	Summary of Events and Information	Remarks and references to Appendices
6/10/17	2.0 About	concentrating several parties of the enemy the nearest being 20 captured. Our casualties were 1 officer and 5 O. Ranks slightly wounded. The normal nightly firing was carried out. A.173 taking the place of A.153. There were in conjunction with the 110th S.A. and the 295th H.A.G. a Gas Shell Bombardment of RIBECOURT was carried out from 12 M.N. to 12.5 A.M.	
7/10/17		The enemy fired 10 rounds 15 c.m. How at the corner of HAVRINCOURT WOOD in R.12.b which he probably is using as a Battery front. Rain all day. Enemy line erased at 10 am and watched out. Put down (?) known.	
8/10/17		The usual hate shells were fired by day. It is reported of the infantry that houses at R.15.a.36.46 and 12.60. by the enemy gun and not bridge at IV Corps boundary was covered at the fallen of the enemy artillery slightly active through the day on YORKSHIRE BANK in R.32.a. during the day the 105 R.I.R. railed (?) the enemy outpost line at R.33.d. 60.20. bringing 1 prisoner and	

Army Form C. 2118.

WAR DIARY
or
INTELLIGENCE SUMMARY.
(Erase heading not required.)

153rd Brigade T.M.
October 1917

Place	Date	Hour	Summary of Events and Information	Remarks and references to Appendices
	8/10/17		[illegible] and supporting infantry in [advance?] on the Enemy. The aerial [illegible] [illegible] no [casualties?] at [illegible]	
	9/10/17		Nothing to report. It is considered inadvisable to [risk?] movement of Marching during the day. It is impossible that an enemy [observer?] taking place on the COMBANK [spur?] [illegible] the front [line?] all [batteries?] of this Brigade [notifying?] [illegible] of the [illegible] Corps and during the night to all approaches to the front line [system?] under enemy fire.	
	10/10/17		During the day and night this was kept up all approaches to the enemy forward system in [occupation?] to the [north?] [right?] of [illegible]	
	11/10/17		[Owing?] to a [time?] lull in the weather, movement was [noted?], enemy plans carry on our work but our [strong?] [response?] to the enemy would [report?] [illegible] no work [carried?] out.	
	12/10/17		Enemy showed a slightly increased activity firing with two [illegible] [illegible] [illegible] in YPRES BANK, to which our T.M. retaliated	

A6945 Wt. W11422/M1160 350,000 12/16 D. D. & L. Forms/C/2118/14.

Army Form C. 2118.

WAR DIARY
or
INTELLIGENCE SUMMARY.
(Erase heading not required.)

153rd Brigade M.G.

October 1917.

Place	Date	Hour	Summary of Events and Information	Remarks and references to Appendices
	12/10/17 Continued		retaliated with effect. The usual night firing was carried out. Batteries of the Divisional Artillery are now registered and the Right Group are covered by all batteries in their Brigade covering the 107th Infantry Brigade and the Right Battalion of the 108th Infantry Brigade is the line.	
	13/10/17		Hostile T.M. fired on YORKSHIRE BANK from K.26.b.5.3. Enemy Aeroplane firing was carried out.	
	14/10/17		Now more aeroplanes really had observer in K.20.a. Hostile aircraft active every morning flying over HAVRINCOURT WOOD. A group of aircraft work was had in front of Head at K.27.d.20.45 seen working in the house. HAVRINCOURT CHURCH north through the line for the first time from O.P. at K.27.b.92.90. HAVRINCOURT TOWER (K.27.b.10.40) appears changed by M.G. fire, left arm very blurry now from Tank Explosion and usual firing carried out.	
	15/10/17		Hostile aircraft active over HAVRINCOURT WOOD in Many sectors. Usual night firing carried out.	

Army Form C. 2118.

WAR DIARY
or
INTELLIGENCE SUMMARY
(Erase heading not required.)

153rd I.B. Brigade B.H.

October 1917

Place	Date	Hour	Summary of Events and Information	Remarks and references to Appendices
	16/10/17		Near enemy observed in trench K.30.c.3.2. One man with rifle seen to leave road at K.22.K.5.6 and walk across to T. Wood at K.26.6.6.4. Hostile aircraft active over our lines between 7.0am & 11pm and again at 3.30 to 4.0 Pm. Night firing carried out as usual.	
	17/10/17		New O.P. observed in K.33.c.65.75. Enemy men repeatedly seen in K.30.c. throughout the day, engaged not by B.153. TM corps knoved. Bombardment preparation for out company (663/K.1) and night firing carried out.	
	18/10/17		A new trench has been dug at K.33.a.92.73. It was camouflaged reported by B.153. Hostile T.M. active on YORKSHIRE BANK fired from SNOWDON at BUGGARTS HOLE. Group Concentration carried out on K.29.c.65.70. C.153 fired on our practical M.G. at K.27.K.39.	
	19/10/17		New wire observed at K.23.c. enemy R.man reported himself on telegraph line at dugout OP about K.26.b.85.30. H.T.M. PERCY active on front line at K.32.d. T.M. obtained by Group Concentration would night firing carried out.	

Army Form C. 2118.

WAR DIARY

~~INTELLIGENCE SUMMARY~~

(Erase heading not required.)

153rd Brigade R.F.A.

October 1917.

Place	Date	Hour	Summary of Events and Information	Remarks and references to Appendices
	20/10/17		Hostile T.M. active in N.W. corner of BOGGARTS HOLE (K.33.b) firing about 12 rounds on YORKSHIRE BANK. Snipers also active in front. Old rounds silenced by our howitzers.	
	21/10/17		The new trench K.33.a appears to have been placed at K. BOGGARTS HOLE. This is still to be seen. A.153 fired on new trench K.33.a - K.27.a. H.T.M. active on our front line at K.32.a from N.W. corner of BOGGARTS HOLE. No fire was drawn by us from "GHS" T.M. firing from BUTLERS CROSS. Q.3 curtails. Usual night firing carried out.	
	22/10/17		New front line trench in course of construction from N.W. corner of BOGGARTS HOLE runs from K.33.b.00.71 - K.27.c. Hostile snipers harassing it R.33.a.F5.93. Salt Pits dug out intended a few yards above it K.33.b.07. Enemy seen to be found to N.W. of front line working there at K.33.b. Own trench mortars with BOGGARTS HOLE. Active all day. K.27.b. Left hand slightly active. H.T.M. PETER fired on own line K.27.b. Left hand N of our trench T.M. H.mm trench mtr fired. Sniped by Scots Bn. Trench mortar. Hostile aircraft on our line at old windmill concentration.	

Army Form C. 2118.

WAR DIARY
INTELLIGENCE SUMMARY.
(Erase heading not required.)

October 1917.   153rd Brigade R.F.A.

Place	Date	Hour	Summary of Events and Information	Remarks and references to Appendices
	23/10/17		Hostile T.M. shelled YORKSHIRE BANK system firing. We retaliated. Good night firing was carried out.	
	24/10/17		Hostile T.M. firing from K.34.b. and BOGGART'S HOLE shelled our front line. We were shelled by our fire for observation on a 'plane.	
	25/10/17		K.29.d. Harassing fire sent up. Firing was carried out. Nw. 6.T. at about K.27.c. 60.10 from the appearance of fresh work seems to have been used by the enemy as O.P. K.23.6.29. M.G. at top Z slope hit. Trench HAMMICOURT MILLNES TO copse. Concentration on K.27.a shelved by one plane. Night firing carried out.	
	26/10/17		Harassing fire programme carried out. Also heavy night firing.	
	27/10/17		Hostile artillery more active. At 12.5 a.m. MN burst about 150 yards NE of RIBECOURT. 100 rounds were also fired at A&C.	
	28/10/17		Harassing fire was normal. Night firing was carried out. At 10.5 p.m. MN burst on Hostile Artillery more active than usual. SHROPSHIRE SPUR B.3.c hit by heavy shells. Throughout front 50% were fired 50 rounds on the large target.	

WAR DIARY / INTELLIGENCE SUMMARY

Army Form C. 2118.

(Erase heading not required.)

153rd Brigade R.F.A.

October 1917

Place	Date	Hour	Summary of Events and Information	Remarks and references to Appendices
	28/10/17		carried out slow normal night firing	
	29/10/17		Hostile 10cm How. fired 100 rounds at Q.3.d. WATER COURSE and OXFORD VALLEY. 30 rounds of 15cm. were fired on Battn H.Q., R.W.C. Branch & this post put in connection with the Hyppogryphs trench. Bombardment Howitzers fire and night firing as ordered out.	
	30/10/17		Hostile planes at an altitude of 2-3000 feet moved on lineage of HAVRINCOURT Town seen behind FLESQUIERES at 2.30 pm nothing noth. Harassing fire and night firing was carried out.	
	31/10/17		Frequent movement at K.29.a.70.70. Hostile artillery quiet. No movement T.M. was firing at (K.34.d.5.f.45) Hostile Batteries were observed from F.30M to 10.30M on BOURLON WOOD. Normal night firing was carried out.	

1/11/17

Chatfield Major
153 Bde RFA

WAR DIARY or INTELLIGENCE SUMMARY

36 DY 153rd Brigade RFA Vol 23
November 1914

Place	Date	Hour	Summary of Events and Information	Remarks and references to Appendices
METZ EN COUTURE	1/11/17	Night 8½-3	Ref. Ref. 8½. Usual night firing carried out on enemy's forward approaches and stores.	
"		Day	Battery position FA1 Q.12.32 shelled with 10.5cm shrap. 200 rds. Minimal hostile artillery activity.	
"	2/11/17	Night 8½-5	Bde. rds. expended on front, rear and approaches to B.30 and R.36. Relieve a local relief was expected. Heavy shelling of infantry occurred during the day. Took taking off the guns detached one section in order to save casualties to personnel and equipment.	
"	3/11/17	11pm	Enemy patrol attempted to enter "B" sec 20 Q.12.30.60. but were repulsed leaving one wounded prisoner in our hands who died shortly after. Increased enemy activity.	
"	4/11/17	Night (3rd/4th)	Raiding party 3 O.R. and 1 Y.O.R. of 1½ York Regt. Horse attacked enemy lines in kind. Normal hostile fire protective barrage for 30 minutes. 1 O.R. Killed 1 O.R. missing 11 O.Rs wounded. Casualties inflicted on enemy. Nil.	

Army Form C. 2118.

WAR DIARY (Cont'd).
or
INTELLIGENCE SUMMARY.

153rd Brigade R.F.A. November 1917

(Erase heading not required.)

Instructions regarding War Diaries and Intelligence Summaries are contained in F. S. Regs., Part II, and the Staff Manual respectively. Title pages will be prepared in manuscript.

Place	Date	Hour	Summary of Events and Information	Remarks and references to Appendices
METZ EN COUTURE	4/11/17	10.30pm	Normal trench warfare. Wire cutting not during the day.	
"	5/11/17		Corps concentration are fired on cross roads in HAVRINCOURT. R2b14. Usual night firing programme was carried out. Evening artillery activity normal during the day showing a slight increase to the right. "HINDENBURG" concentration carried out.	
"	6/11/17		Heavy enemy trench mortar activity impossible. A/153 carried out calibration. Night firing by lone guns.	
"	7/11/17		Great increase in hostile artillery activity. Enemy 500 shells of different calibre were fired on left Battalion 104th Inf. Brigade between 10pm & midnight. Enemy concentration not over fired. Area taken in hand to by RA at 11.45pm 12.30am and 1.30am	
"	8/11/17		Increased artillery shown by FA's also attempted to carry on our but was driven back by AA and MG fire from and enemy artillery normal.	
"	9/11/17	SOS signal 2.45 am	SOS signal sent up by Rocket Guard. Batteries opened fire on 'I' Lay Zone. Fire was carried on for four minutes when information was received that friends were there but not been lost two pigeon by RE	

A6945 Wt. W14422/M1160 350,000 12/16 D. D. & L. Forms/C./2118/14.

WAR DIARY
or
INTELLIGENCE SUMMARY.

(Erase heading not required.)

Army Form C. 2118.

153rd Brigade RFA
November 1917
(3)

Place	Date	Hour	Summary of Events and Information	Remarks and references to Appendices
METZ EN COUTURE	10.11.17		Hostile artillery below normal activity. Harassing fire programme not carried out during the night.	
"	11.11.17		Hostile artillery inactive all day. 16 formation of 6 EA's crossed our lines about 1 pm and were engaged by AA guns and MG's and were driven back, one machine appeared to have a forced landing in its own line. C/153 carried out calibration in conjunction with 3rd Field Survey Coy RE's. Results satisfactory. Visual might firing was carried out. Hostile artillery nil again all day. Firing normal.	
"	12.11.17		" " " " " " " " "	
"	13.11.17		At 3:45 pm an EA totally lost control its way in the mist and ran out of petrol landed by C/153's position in Q.21.a. Pilot was taken prisoner and sent machine remained by RFC. Pilot states that the enemy from LAON was taught he was behind his own lines when he landed.	
"	14.11.17		Nothing of importance occurred all day.	

WAR DIARY or INTELLIGENCE SUMMARY

Army Form C. 2118.

153rd Brigade R.F.A.
November 1914

(Erase heading not required.)

Instructions regarding War Diaries and Intelligence Summaries are contained in F. S. Regs., Part II. and the Staff Manual respectively. Title pages will be prepared in manuscript.

Place	Date	Hour	Summary of Events and Information	Remarks and references to Appendices
METZ EN COUTURE	15.11.17		Enemy artillery in action all day. 10 p.m. fired 200 ms into infantry SPOIL HEAP K200. 3.0 p.m. Battery turn moved to standings in HAPLINCOURT	
	16.11.17		Nothing of importance occurred all day.	
	17.11.17	10 p.m.	One section of B/153 moved to forward position at CLAYTON CROSS Rd.	
		5.30 a.m.	Enemy under cover of heavy artillery preparation carried F. Sap. Q4a and was successful in capturing 4 O.R's of 1st R.I.F. Right Sect. fired on Normal S.O.S. followed S.O.S. "B" D & R.A. Stand down given at 5.56 a.m.	
	18.11.17		Slight increase in hostile artillery activity in the vicinity of TRESCAULT. Local enemy fire carried out.	
	19.11.17		Nothing of importance occurred during the day. During the night remainder of 153rd Brigade moved into positions along HUBERT ROAD Q8a. Hostile firing could not on usual scale but E... enemy suspicious on the part of recovery	

WAR DIARY or INTELLIGENCE SUMMARY

Army Form C. 2118.

153rd Brigade RFA

November 1917

Place	Date	Hour	Summary of Events and Information	Remarks and references to Appendices
METZ EN COUTURE	20.11.17	6.20am	First day of advance. Zero hour. Flesquières-Havrincourt line attack mostly by tanks. Our tank guns to Flesquières did not meet much trouble and set up for about 8½ hrs. Whole troops fired chiefly against right of our left outpost line. 9.30 major lines moved up further (Havrincourt) and Sgt. Muriel acted up Roads very congested. 8.30 orders cancelled with reference to advance from MFZ. Direct road not brigade ordered to proceed to position to supply our attack on INCHY-EN-ARTOIS. 12 midnight 153rd Brigade leave vicinity of MFZ and proceed via RUYAULCOURT, HERMIES and DEMICOURT to new position.	
HERMIES	21.11.17	4.30	Her arrived at WINDY mansions CORNER J29 central. Position to K5 and reconnoitred and 1.30 batteries move forward to positions. North artillery quiet. HQ established in late front line trench. Kite during the night between front lines.	

WAR DIARY or INTELLIGENCE SUMMARY.

Army Form C. 2118.

153rd Brigade R.F.A.

November 1917

Place	Date	Hour	Summary of Events and Information	Remarks and references to Appendices
S.F. of DEMICOURT J.18	23:11:17	?	Enemy make small counter attack but are repulsed by artillery barrage before reaching our line. Enemy artillery fact quiet. No night firing by B.218. Wagon lines at WINDY CORNER	
"	23:11:17	10 Am	Attack with tanks on MOEUVRES. Great increase in hostile artillery barrage. Tanks appeared to go overhead. Breakdowns but Inf. attack unsuccessful. Light enemy fire carried out.	
"	24:11:17	10.20 am	Enemy attack BOURLON village. Batteries fire on "BOURLON S.O.S." Enemy held but use all through attack with aircraft observation. Casualties to personnel and two guns damaged.	
"		3.30 pm	10th E Inf. Brigade withdrawn & barrage attack HINDENBURG support trenches in FIS9H and Sat Feb19. Tanks do operate covered by smoke barrage. Attack unsuccessful. No night firing by 153 Bde.	
	25:11:17		Nothing event and unsuccessful.	
		3 pm	Battalion fired on TADPOLE S.O.S. inspecting enemy counter attack which did not take place.	

153rd Brigade RFA
Army Form C. 2118.

WAR DIARY
INTELLIGENCE SUMMARY
(Erase heading not required.)

November 1917

Place	Date	Hour	Summary of Events and Information	Remarks and references to Appendices
SE of DEMICOURT K15†	26/11/17	—	Harassing fire and registration carried out as usual. Enemy hostile artillery normal. Right Sect.	
	27/11/17	6.20	Attack on BOURLON and FONTAINE - very rainy morning. Although attack unsuccessful 2pm. enemy put down heavy barrage on our lines in front of MOEUVRES. 153rd Brigade fired "CEMETERY S.O.S." 153rd Brigade and 143rd Brigade from left group when LT/Col Simpson 155th Brigade HQ were in position. B Lock 1 in K15a. Right Section fired 50 rds harried front to position in rge. B/153 WL moved to position then HARMks and rather BQ4.	
	28/11/17	4am	C/153 moved to position in rge. B/153 WL moved to position.	
		4pm	B/153 moved to position in rge alongside C/153. Night firing carried out as usual.	
	29/11/17		Nothing of importance occurred. HA normal.	

WAR DIARY 153rd Brigade R.F.A.
or
INTELLIGENCE SUMMARY.

November 1917

Army Form C. 2118.

Place	Date	Hour	Summary of Events and Information	Remarks and references to Appendices
S.W. of LOCK 4 KISA	30-11-17	8.30	Enemy launched big counter attack from BOURLON to MOEUVRES many large parties of Germans were caught in the open by artillery fire. 153rd Bde fired S.O.S. barrage throughout the day expending approx. 10,000 rds. Attack was completely repulsed by m.g. and artillery fire. It is estimated that two German divisions were thrown in the attack. Many aeroplane encounters took place during the day mainly in the downfall of many enemy machines on both sides. Normal conditions were resumed about 6.30 p.m. Right harassing fire was carried out as usual. Brigade suffered no casualties.	

Army Form C. 2118.

WAR DIARY
INTELLIGENCE SUMMARY. 183rd Brigade R.F.A.

December 1917

(Erase heading not required.)

Place	Date	Hour	Summary of Events and Information	Remarks and references to Appendices
Ref Sheet 57C R.14.b.9.4.	1st Decr 1917		Normal unusual gun: hostile Artillery activity. Normal Operation for Brigade O.P. was noisy with 1.47 hr, 9 pm. C/L Thompson N.C.O. C/183rd Brigade R.F.A (and B/153rd Brigade R.F.A) being killed. During 2.40 pm the enemy attacked our Infantry between MOEUVRES and TADPOLE COPSE but was repulsed. Night normal. The enemy looking for crews out by night.	
ditto	2nd Decr 1917		Hostile Artillery showed increased activity especially in the back areas. C/183rd Brigade R.F.A suffered 40 casualties at Rores and numerous casualties occurred in the battery positions. The lugger O.P. B. Holland R.F.A. 1/J/153rd Brigade R.F.A. was again shelled, 2/Lieut B.S. Holland R.F.A. 1/J/153rd B. R.F.A. being killed. It was decided to move the O.P. 8.45 p.m. the also suffered 10 casualties at the gun line. At 7.45 pm the S.O.S. signal was sent up by the MOEUVRES outpost following a heavy bombardment the enemy again attacked our Infantry between MOEUVRES and TADPOLE COPSE but was repulsed by rifle and machine gun fire supporting heavy barrage fire through being covered thence heavy barrage fire by Bigede.	

M6945. Wt. W14422/M1160. 350,000 12/16 D.D.&L. Forms/C/2118/14.

WAR DIARY or INTELLIGENCE SUMMARY.

Army Form C. 2118.

153rd Brigade R.F.A.

(Erase heading not required.)

Place	Date	Hour	Summary of Events and Information	Remarks and references to Appendices
Ref Sh 57c NE Sh 1 9/4	30 Nov 1917		During daylight the day was uneventful with the exception these being C/153rd Brigade R.F.A. were shelled suffering slight casualties. About 11:30 pm the enemy put down a barrage on our gun line system. From BOURLON to MOEUVRES following this he attempted to front the position but was repulsed. Signs given have having fy Covered Out. 2/Lieut K.I. Scott joined the Brigade	
	4 Dec 1917		Orders received with regard to the evacuation of the BOURLON SALIENT. Positions South of HERMIES reconnoitred from Battery Positions chosen. Normal activity during the evening. Lts Echo b and g receiving offensive attention. flank Battery positions selection fight given to opposing the crowd and then unimpeded reformable to one withdrawal of 193rd Brigade R.F.A. Infantry position during the night of Dec 4/5 our Brigade in the line was relieved by one brigade covering the two brigades fronts. Orders that line assembled and a strong outpost line put out. Lines moved to O.6.d	

WAR DIARY or INTELLIGENCE SUMMARY

Army Form C. 2118.

153rd Brigade R.F.A.

Place	Date	Hour	Summary of Events and Information	Remarks and references to Appendices
Ref Sheet 57 D S.E. R.n. F.9.4	5th Dec 1917		Hostile Artillery quiet during the morning. Increased activity as the day wore on. During the day many hostile light were engaged by 18 Pdr and 4.5" How. Attacking party consisted on the Enemy as any approached the site of our old organised front line. Headquarters established in old position of 11/3rd Brigade R.F.A. after position J.30.c.v.0 South of HERMIES by 9am between commenced by withdrawn to position South of HERMIES. J.30.d. Our C Augustin retired in new position by 1am. On withdrawal our complete and batteries were not touched in new position. Hostile artillery did not interfere with withdrawal.	
J.30.c.0.0.	6th Dec 1917		Day uneventful and no movement of any enemy troops observed. Batteries spent day in digging position & 1853 cleaned out position of ammunition and supply 14 Cures Blitz and gun pits and 6 horses came transporting for Cured on by night.	

Army Form C. 2118.

WAR DIARY
153rd Brigade R.F.A.
INTELLIGENCE SUMMARY.
Part II.

(Erase heading not required.)

Place	Date	Hour	Summary of Events and Information	Remarks and references to Appendices
Shw S.9.C. T.E. T.30.c.00.	7th December 1917		Positions were reconnoitred for and each battery sent forward one gun to an advanced gun position in order to deal with any tanks in the event of enemy using same. Batteries did some registration. Hostile Artillery did not show much activity. Enemy Aircraft also inactive. Usual harassing fire carried out by night.	
do.	8th Dec 1917		Heavy Artillery active down HAVRINCOURT and FLESQUIERES. Day uneventful. Usual harassing fire and registration carried out in the morning. Nearly in the afternoon. During the night the enemy attempted several minor bombing attacks on our outposts and patrols, but these were driven off in each case. Usual night harassing fire carried out.	
do.	9th Dec 1917		Hostile Artillery showed more activity than usual but no damage done. A.S.S.O.S. guns on standby were cleared but no damage done. B.S.O.S. guns on S.O.S lines for 1½ hours. Very heavy firing carried out as usual.	
do.	10th Dec 1917		Patrols a long way out. Enemy Aeroplanes crossed over lines	

Instructions regarding War Diaries and Intelligence Summaries are contained in F. S. Regs., Part II. and the Staff Manual respectively. Title pages will be prepared in manuscript.

5

WAR DIARY
or
INTELLIGENCE SUMMARY.
(Erase heading not required.)

153rd Brigade RFA

Army Form C. 2118.

Place	Date	Hour	Summary of Events and Information	Remarks and references to Appendices
Sheet 57C	10th Dec 1917		flying at a very low altitude. The formation consisted of a fighting escort of scouts and one or two large bombs dropping machines. They met with no opposition from either the AA guns or R.F.C. The formation proceeded to the Wagon Line area and dropped a large quantity of different sized bombs again without interference on the part of our R.F.C. The formation eventually broke up and went home separately having suffered no casualties. Large number of hostile observation balloons up. No event of importance during the day and batteries carried out normal day firing on chosen targets. Night firing carried out on selected targets. H.V. guns shelled Headquarters & Wagon Line area. No damage done.	
R.6				
J.30.c.0				
do	11th Dec 1917		Orders received regarding the exchange of personnel of the 153rd, 312th and 235th Brigades. In the morning the Colonel reconnoitred Battery positions and Headquarters in K.29 and K.36. No accommodation of any sort for personnel of batteries. Officer of 312th Brigade visited batteries in order to become conversant with tactical situation. At 3-45 pm ~~[illegible]~~ O.P. reported S.O.S. in R.9.b. where GRAINCOURT ROAD crosses the CANAL DU NORD. Batteries opened fire in response to call and continued firing for 15 minutes. Hostile artillery showed normal activity during the day.	
do	12th Dec 1917		Exchange of personnel ~~between~~ between 153rd Brigade RFA and 312th Reserve RFA carried out 3 at a time leaving sufficient men in each position to man all guns. Relief completed by 6 pm. Headquarters moved to dugouts in HINDENBURG LINE K.34.d.	

A5834 Wt. W4973/M687 750,000 8/16 D. D. & L. Ltd. Forms/C.2118/13.

WAR DIARY
INTELLIGENCE SUMMARY

Army Form C. 2118.

13th Brigade R.F.A.

Place	Date	Hour	Summary of Events and Information	Remarks and references to Appendices
N.E. of Rue d	12th Jan 1917 (continued)		Although enemy did not reply rate relief troops were carried out. 13th Brigade carried out the observation of enemy battery and some MG & Rifle fire was CG 24th Brigade R.F.A.	
"	13th Jan 1917		Found all 4 of the canal and gun emplaced and not done on position. Fire taken over with Brigade to gun site.	
"	14th Jan 1917		Looked to improve battery positions. We had 1st Brigade R.F.A. Some trenches & casualties no one wounded. We were encountered complete with roads and good stores in which we were returned by 6 other Batteries. Batteries on dugouts on K.9.d.0.0 by Barny R.F.A. who had 153rd Battery R.F.A. one in and 150th Brigade R.F.A. out for sept.6 entry. Brigade 14th January to Manorim 36 & horses.	
Rue de l	15th Jan 1917		The day was a reputation and extending down in the Southern divergency was carried out by night the enemy of Franken	
"	16th Jan 1917		The enemy shewed unusual activity during the day in the neighbourhood of battery positions but no serious damage was caused.	

Army Form C. 2118.

WAR DIARY
or
INTELLIGENCE SUMMARY.

(Erase heading not required.)

10th Bde. R.F.A.

Instructions regarding War Diaries and Intelligence Summaries are contained in F. S. Regs., Part II. and the Staff Manual respectively. Title pages will be prepared in manuscript.

Place	Date	Hour	Summary of Events and Information	Remarks and references to Appendices
R.K.A.20 (contd)	16th Dec 1917		Enemy active all day over front positions. Harassing fire carried out by night.	
do	17th Dec 1917		Enemy and our artillery active. Enemy gassed our front line area & firing by day and Harassing fire by night. Very quiet.	
do	18th Dec 1917		Day very quiet. Arras day and night harassing fire carried out. Z Battery R.F.A. the Brigade went into billets for the night 18/19th inst, relieved by [illegible]	
do	19th Nov 1917		Headquarters moved to Q.12.a.15.60 and Bde. HQ. on Cinema Camp. 3rd Division relieved by 31st Div. & 15th Bde. to 93rd Brigade R.F.A. and B.C. [illegible] at 10 a.m. 153rd Brigade R.F.A. Z Battery R.F.A. and 448 Howitzer Battery relieved by [illegible] & rest on [illegible] roads [illegible]	
Q.12.a.15.60	20th Dec 1917		Day and night very quiet. My guns and my Howitzer fire high and very low. Carried out.	
do	21st Dec 1917		Day quiet. [illegible] patterns Enemy signal activity on [illegible]. Day [illegible] front trench systems [illegible] not [illegible] [illegible] Enemy [illegible] over our gun [illegible] line [illegible] hostile fire by [illegible] gas [illegible] Officer [illegible]	
do	22nd Dec 1917		[illegible] by [illegible] gas [illegible] now [illegible] gone by [illegible] [illegible] check fire	

Army Form C. 2118.

WAR DIARY
or
INTELLIGENCE SUMMARY.
(Erase heading not required.)

1st Brigade R.F.A

Instructions regarding War Diaries and Intelligence Summaries are contained in F.S. Regs., Part II. and the Staff Manual respectively. Title pages will be prepared in manuscript.

Place	Date	Hour	Summary of Events and Information	Remarks and references to Appendices
Brassens	22nd Dec 1917 (continued)		[illegible handwritten entry referring to 63rd Division, relief by 7/8th Brigade, etc.]	
"	23rd Dec 1917		[illegible handwritten entry mentioning METZ-en-COUTURE, wire, battery positions, etc.]	
"	24th Dec 1917	night	[illegible handwritten entry]	
"	25 Dec 1917		Xmas day. Some mail & Xmas greetings.	
"	26 Dec 1917		Hy Day. Frost and cold. 38th Divisional Artillery relieved by 63rd Divisional Artillery. Took over as far as firing line & limber.	
Le Transloy	27th Dec 1917		36th Divisional Artillery [illegible] at Sapigne area.	
"	28th Dec 1917		[illegible]	
"	29th Dec 1917		Hard frost with cold wind. Enemy aeroplanes flew over close to Sapigne. 36 Divisional Artillery over all night.	

A5834 Wt.W4973/M687 750,000 8/16 D.D.&L. Ltd. Forms/C.2118/13.

WAR DIARY
or
INTELLIGENCE SUMMARY.

Army Form C. 2118.

10th August 1919

Place	Date	Hour	Summary of Events and Information	Remarks and references to Appendices
In rendez-vous	29/8/19		Movement halted owing to fog	
"	30/8/19		Fresh slightly hilly but stiff country. Enemy retreat and performed 1917 destruction thoroughly. Advance to TREUX for one night, then to ENNEMAIN, then to Bny. Grande Priele, to have fresh bridge over two places on coy. CAMBRAI front.	
"	31/8/19		French Div held with only slight fire very heavy artillery fire at 1 am and 5 am.	

Signed W.B. Kew
Major R.H.A.
Commanding 103rd Brigade R.H.A.

Army Form C. 2118.

WAR DIARY
INTELLIGENCE SUMMARY.
(Erase heading not required.)

153rd Brigade R.F.A.

9 M 25

Place	Date	Hour	Summary of Events and Information	Remarks and references to Appendices
Immater	August 1918		153rd Brigade R.F.A. marched to Vieil-Sur-Essue	
Vieil-Sur-Essue	2nd Aug 1918		153rd Brigade R.F.A. marched to Hamel	
Hamel	3rd Aug		153rd Brigade R.F.A. at Hamel	
do	4th Aug		do	
do	5th Aug		do	
do	6th Aug		do	
do	7th Aug		153rd Brigade R.F.A. marched to Hangest	
Hangest	8th Aug		153rd Brigade R.F.A. at Hangest	
do	9th Aug		do	
do	10th Aug		153rd Brigade R.F.A. marched to Roye	
Roye	11th Aug		153rd Brigade R.F.A. at Roye	
do	12th Aug		153rd Brigade R.F.A. moved to Bezy. St Christopher. Commenced taking over from 6 French Divisionne Artillery. 1am of an Battery at position:- One Gun B Battery A.14.a. 40.55. C Battery A.14.a. 50.80. F16C. 87.90. B Battery A.14.a. 40.70. D Battery A.14.a. 40.70. sent into action in position	

Army Form C. 2118.

WAR DIARY
INTELLIGENCE SUMMARY. 103rd Brigade RFA
(Erase heading not required.)

Instructions regarding War Diaries and Intelligence Summaries are contained in F. S. Regs., Part II. and the Staff Manual respectively. Title pages will be prepared in manuscript.

Place	Date	Hour	Summary of Events and Information	Remarks and references to Appendices
Sus 25 A.	13th January 1918		Headquarters taken over from Sumer at F.22.a.8.3.	
F.22.a.8.3	14th January		Remainder of Brigade came into action. 103rd Brigade RFA becomes Left Group, 36th Divisional Artillery consisting of L.S.B.C. and D. Batteries 153rd Brigade R.F.A. and 68th Battery R.F.A. 14th Army Field Artillery Brigade. Hostile Battery guns sweeping machine gun Stations.	
	15th January		Visibility had owing to heavy ghost mist. Hostile Artillery guns sweeping machine gun Stations. Visibility bad owing to mist.	
	16th January		Registration commenced. Hostile Artillery guns Visibility	
	17th January		Registration against Crown and Anchor Battery guns Visibility. Very no day.	
	18th January		Registration on known points in the Sector Carried out with good results. Small parties of the Enemy were observed on the road in B.6.d and B.2.e. and engaged by 4 an 18 Pdrs with effect. Our airships were active over the Enemy lines all day.	

Army Form C. 2118.

WAR DIARY
INTELLIGENCE SUMMARY
(Erase heading not required.)

153rd Brigade R.F.A.

Place	Date	Hour	Summary of Events and Information	Remarks and references to Appendices
F.22.d.8.3.	19th Jany (Contd from previous)		Visibility fair. Registration and calibration continued & numbers of Enemy hostile batties were observed and dispersed by our fire. Several enemy planes flying high over our lines were engaged by our A.A. & M.G.s and driven off. Hostile Artillery almost inactive. Fine warm sunny day.	
do.	20th January.		Fire in the vicinity of CASTRES. Visibility good all day. Registration and checking of S.O.S. Line carried out by Batteries. Hostile Artillery fairly active. Several rounds of H.V. gun and 10.5cm fell in our forward area. Spoken Red. and Green lights and Very lights were sent up during fours on the side of St Quentin by the enemy apparently from Sucré. No apparent action was taken. Conditions unfavorable for aircraft. Visibility dull but improving slightly towards afternoon.	
do.	21st January.		Registration and Calibration continued. Slight enemy shelling of our forward system around Visibility good.	

Army Form C. 2118.

WAR DIARY
or
INTELLIGENCE SUMMARY.
(Erase heading not required.)

153rd Brigade R.F.A.

Instructions regarding War Diaries and Intelligence Summaries are contained in F. S. Regs., Part II. and the Staff Manual respectively. Title pages will be prepared in manuscript.

Place	Date	Hour	Summary of Events and Information	Remarks and references to Appendices
	22nd Jany (continued)			
F.22.a.8.3			Offrs. Fortis Battery Guns, Hostile Aircraft inactive. Our Aircraft fairly active over Enemy lines during good visibility. Visibility bad all day except for about 1 hour in the afternoon when it improved slightly.	
"	23rd Jany		Enemy movement considerably above normal. Several working parties were engaged by our 18 pdrs with good results. Hostile Artillery quiet. Weather conditions unfavourable for Aircraft & ground. Hostile Trench mortars active all day and frequent Flare alarms.	
"	24th Jany		Registration and Calibration continued with good results. Our and Enemy Aircraft very active. Enemy Planes crossed our lines in a great height. State Artillery normal. Visibility good most of the day.	
D.	25th Jany		Enemy Army & other wires and Observation being important no attempt has been made and our Aircraft inactive.	
"	26th Jany		Visibility good most morning all day. Our Aircraft fair. Enemy our Aircraft inactive	

Army Form. C. 2118.

WAR DIARY
of
INTELLIGENCE SUMMARY.
(Erase heading not required.)

153rd Brigade R.F.A.

Place	Date	Hour	Summary of Events and Information	Remarks and references to Appendices
F.22.d.8.3.	22nd January		Registration and Calibration continued. Artillery normal. The Enemy bombarded our trenches slightly with 5.9 C. On aircraft active normal. Enemy raided the Enemy's lines and put on his trenches Artillery barrage were active. Enemy attempted to cross our lines but were immediately engaged by our Inf.y. troops and driven off. At 9 p.m. the Right Battalion of the Regt. Brigade reported that the Enemy were in their front line. Front line was reinforced and C/153rd Brigade R.F.A. and 66th Battery R.F.A. fired on their S.O.S. lines. Our patrol was encountered in S.29.C. and one Officer and 1 other rank are missing. At 9.30 p.m. Situation became normal & so far as can be ascertained our casualties were 2 O.Rs. Ranks wounded. Visibility very good all day.	
	23rd January		Calibration again carried out but both unsatisfactory results owing to bad visibility. In the afternoon an Enemy working party observed in B.1.d.50.96. was engaged by our 18 Pdrs. with	

D. D. & L., London, E.C.
(A7893) Wt. W19/M1672 350,000 4/17 Sch. 52a Forms C/2118/14

Army Form C. 2118.

WAR DIARY
or
INTELLIGENCE SUMMARY.

(Erase heading not required.)

152nd Brigade R.F.A.

Instructions regarding War Diaries and Intelligence
Summaries are contained in F. S. Regs., Part II.
and the Staff Manual respectively. Title pages
will be prepared in manuscript.

Place	Date	Hour	Summary of Events and Information	Remarks and references to Appendices
F.22.d.8.3.	28 January		Our Artillery normal. Hostile Artillery more active. About 60 rounds 77 m.m. and 105 m.m. fire in on forward system. Our Aircraft and the Enemy's very active. The Enemy fired about 2 R.E. An enemy plane flying low over our lines was engaged by one of our R.E.8's and fire to flight. Between 8 and 8.40 p.m. formations of enemy aircraft passed over our lines and Enemy bombs were dropped.	
do	29 January		Our Artillery active. Hostile Artillery sky active. About 50 rounds 77 m.m. and 105 m.m. being fired into our forward system. Our Aircraft and the Enemy's very active all day. 1 of our planes was forced to ground near Roupy. Between 8.45 p.m. and 12 Midnight large formations of enemy planes again came over our lines and dropped a number of bombs.	
do	30 January		Our Enemy Enemy Enemy patrols were observed, engaged by our 18 Pdrs and dispersed. Hostile Artillery fairly active. About 50 rounds fell in our forward system. Hostile Aircraft very active all.	

D. D. & L., London, E.C.
(A5832) Wt. W20/M1672 350,000 4/17 Sch 92a Forms/C/2118/14

Army Form C. 2118.

WAR DIARY
or
INTELLIGENCE SUMMARY.
(Erase heading not required.)

153rd Brigade R.F.A.

Instructions regarding War Diaries and Intelligence Summaries are contained in F. S. Regs., Part II. and the Staff Manual respectively. Title pages will be prepared in manuscript.

Place	Date	Hour	Summary of Events and Information	Remarks and references to Appendices
F.22.d.8.3.	30 January (continued)		day. On average however, S. section fired two rounds on St. Quentin Cabaret Line and another on the Belgian Battery 9 pm and 1 am. [illegible] fired fourteen Zarnoff shells over [illegible] road and duff many [illegible] in [illegible] front [illegible] [illegible]	
	31 January		Enemy fired [illegible] trenches as day and provided observation posts. Hostile [illegible] quiet. Except [illegible] [illegible] [illegible]	

[signature] Major R.F.A.
Commanding 153rd Brigade R.F.A.

Army Form C. 2118.

WAR DIARY
or
INTELLIGENCE SUMMARY.
(Erase heading not required.)

153rd Brigade R.F.A.

February

Place	Date	Hour	Summary of Events and Information	Remarks and references to Appendices
Aux G2B.5	1/2/18		The quiet on the whole sector continues. Batteries are doing practically no shooting except calibration and no enemy working parties are engaged unless they are of 20 or more in number. The batteries are firmly engaged in strengthening the positions they are at present occupying, building alternative positions for occupation in event of being shelled out and building a head position which will be occupied by Beginning Batteries in the event of the enemy launching an attack on this front.	
F23.d.8.5.	2/2/18		Enemy Aircraft during hours of observation are active over our lines and at night bombed wagon lines and rear areas. No casualties were suffered. Hostile shelling during the day was quiet and the only shelling reported was registration.	
	3/2/18		Registration and calibration was continued by batteries on PIREPUER and LA BIETTE. Day very quiet and with the exception of nights bombing by the enemy no hostile activity was displayed	
	4/2/18		Day quiet. A few rounds of light trench mortar were fired into our lines in B.8.C. A little registration and calibration was carried out by the batteries	

Army Form C. 2118.

WAR DIARY
INTELLIGENCE SUMMARY

(Erase heading not required.)

152nd Brigade R.F.A.

February

Place	Date	Hour	Summary of Events and Information	Remarks and references to Appendices
Sheet 62B S.23.d.	5/2/18		Feeling of unrest occurred during the day. Visibility was impaired owing to mist and no activity was shown on either side. The work on reinforcing positions continues.	
F.23.d.8.5.	6/2/18		The enemy ranging batteries were dispersed to firing at B.2.c.30.70 and B.1.d.70.30. A few rifle grenades were fired into our front line at B.Y.b.70.09 at 2.5 a.m.	
	7/2/18		Owing to bad observation no shooting was performed by Batteries except the destruction of an enemy working party at B.1.d.9.5.60 an 8.30 am. by the infantry. Enemy trench light signalling was seen from ST. QUENTIN cathedral during the night. Y.1.* Visibility almost nil.	
	8/2/18		Nothing of interest occurred during the day.	
	9/2/18		General movement throughout the day by enemy working parties are engaged by our batteries and machine guns. Trench mortars. Several rounds of 77mm gun and 105 hows fire in OESTRES CASTRE and front trench systems. Enemy aircraft are active between 8am. and 10am.	
	10/2/18		There is continuous movement on top of trenches from B.1.c.3.5. to B.1.b.4.8. Also a great deal of transport is being used. Artillery activity on either side. There was slight aircraft activity on both sides.	

Army Form C. 2118.

WAR DIARY
INTELLIGENCE SUMMARY.

(Erase heading not required.)

February 153rd Brigade R.F.A.

Place	Date	Hour	Summary of Events and Information	Remarks and references to Appendices
Rest B2B F23 d & S.	11/2/18		Slight aircraft activity after noon on both sides. Between groups of the enemy airships hostile batteries. Several groups of the enemy are reported conducting themselves in a similar manner really doing nothing but attempting to after was indecisive. Others were firing steel frames round a gun in a case for 2 hours without any loss of life. Working party was engaged by an 18 Pdr. with effect. Hostile artillery quiet except for the shelling of CASTRES by a 150mm Battery. There was little enemy movement observed throughout the day. A Coy L.Tr.M. working party on the Morcheim Line.	
	12/2/18		Des. SINGES. B.1.a. was shelled by an enemy 150mm Battery. No other enemy operations occurred during the day. Observation impossible owing to mist.	
	13/2/18		Slight activity of the enemy system by the enemy during the morning. The enemy working party in B.1.c. was engaged and dispersed.	
	14/2/18		Nothing further in B.1.c. were engaged and dispersed. Several rounds 77mm and 105mm fell in CASTRES and front line.	

Army Form C. 2118.

WAR DIARY
INTELLIGENCE SUMMARY.
(Erase heading not required.)

Army: February 153rd Brigade R.F.A.

Instructions regarding War Diaries and Intelligence Summaries are contained in F. S. Regs., Part II. and the Staff Manual respectively. Title pages will be prepared in manuscript.

Place	Date	Hour	Summary of Events and Information	Remarks and references to Appendices
Sh.62.B 15/2/18 (cont.) F23d&b 16/2/18			systems. Allowed quiet. Registration continued of working party of about 30 men observed on B.1.t. was fired on and dispersed. Between 6pm and 7pm a fraction of enemy flare landed the rail head. Registration continued. Shots fired by above reported. Occasional rounds fire in on from system during the day. Between 8pm and 9pm 150 rounds 150mm fell in G.6 Central, Probably on troops either resting or passing for enemy flares have been seen to fall in fields.	
	17/2/18		Registration of enemy flares again confirmed. Frequent movements on the tramway of Hamel fortin in T.26.d. and B.1.t. with it. Shots fired by 2 guns of No. 5 rounds from a heavy enemy flare section. Near tractor & trucks near G.R.6.15.5. Shots flares fairly active throughout day. About 1pm on one of our observation balloons was brought down by enemy aircraft.	
	18/2/18		T.2.S.d. was fired on and destruction of Goldsmans work. Flare in this platoon taps containing 430mm and tracks fell 4.45am. Opes reserve of the 153rd Brigade R.F.A. being unable to be relieved in the line by the 148th Brigade R.F.A. 30 Division. 1 section of each battery retained.	

Army Form C. 2118.

WAR DIARY
or
INTELLIGENCE SUMMARY.

(Erase heading not required.)

153rd Brigade R.F.A

February

Place	Date	Hour	Summary of Events and Information	Remarks and references to Appendices
Sans C.B. F.2.d.8.5.	20/2/18		Nothing of importance occurred during the day. The night the enemy continuing the bombardment of the battery we retired and Brigade proceeded to OFFOY.	
OFFOY.	21/2/18		Brigade at OFFOY. Having Commanding of Guns Orders Separating Rolling Stores etc Commenced.	
"	22/2/18		Brigade at OFFOY. Moving continued.	
"	23/2/18		do	
"	24/2/18		do	
"	25/2/18		do	
"	26/2/18		do	
"	27/2/18		do	
"	28/2/18		At 11.30am orders recd to move Battery positions at:- Headquarters GRAND SERRAUCOURT. A/153. G.8.D.90.50. B/153. G.8.S.a.9.9. and V.L.S.a.4.9. C/153. L.4.a.4.4. and G.9.t.o.5. D/153. G.9.t. S.S.37. and L.12.c.9.1. Batteries all in position by 9 pm.	

[signature]
Lieut., R.F.A.,
K¹ Adjutant 153rd Brigade, R.F.A.

[signature]
for Lt. Col. R.A.
Commanding 153rd Brigade R.F.A.
attached 152nd

36th Divisional Artillery.

153rd BRIGADE R. F. A.

M A R C H   1 9 1 8

WAR DIARY or INTELLIGENCE SUMMARY

153rd Brigade R.F.A.

Place	Date	Hour	Summary of Events and Information	Remarks and references to Appendices
Gd Seraucourt	1/3/18 to 20/3		Batteries of the Brigade are now in Battle Zone positions as follows:— A/153 G8d 9050 (4 guns) G9b 3030 (2 guns) B/153 G15a 99 (4 guns) L25a 77 (2 guns) C/153 L4a 44 (") G9b 05 (") D/153 G9b 5537 (2 ") L12c 91 (4 ") Headquarters in Grand Seraucourt. During the period work was carried out by batteries on their respective battle zone positions and working parties were found by batteries for the Unoccupied positions. Nothing of importance occurred.	(a) FRANCE
	21/3	4.35am	Enemy offensive opened with very heavy bombardment on our front line. Difficulty was experienced in getting wires through from forward positions as cable routes had been cut by enemy fire. At 7.30am it was apparent that the enemy had reached the Eastern edge of Gd Seraucourt. J.H.Q. were therefore moved back to approx G15a 99. At 10pm instructions received from the R.A. J.H.Q. were moved back to Brig. St. Christophe. Batt'ys were in action between Brig. St. Christophe and Aubigny covering 1085d Junky. B. Le.	
	22/3	2pm	J.H.Q. moved to Pithon and at 8.30pm to Eppeville and by day & night	
	23/3	3am	Batteries rendezvoused at X Rds South of Offoy Batteries in action at Bacquencourt	

Army Form C. 2118.

WAR DIARY
or
INTELLIGENCE SUMMARY.

(Erase heading not required.)

Instructions regarding War Diaries and Intelligence Summaries are contained in F. S. Regs., Part II. and the Staff Manual respectively. Title pages will be prepared in manuscript.

Place	Date	Hour	Summary of Events and Information	Remarks and references to Appendices
Bacquencourt I 35	23/3/18	7 am	The enemy having crossed the river Somme at HAM batteries were withdrawn from Bacquencourt and matched to take up position at U23a 2070. White batteries were withdrawn from 178th Brigade RFA.	SHEET 66D. FRANCE 1:40,000
Flavy le Meldeur V5		5.30 pm	Batteries came into action near FLAVY-LE-MELDEUR	
	24/3/18	3.30 am	Batteries were temporarily withdrawn to near ROUYREL FARM in V.9.b owing to a gap not to enemy had broken through our outpost line and Lt. Colonel GORANCOURT (U.19.d.2.5.)	
		7.10 am	Batteries returned to their position in FLAVY-LE-MELDEUX and — field and OLANCOURT and BONNEUIL CHATEAU (P.29.c)	
FRENICHES		6 pm	The enemy having pressed back the outposts a new night position was ordered. Batteries came into action about 1800 hrs E. & W. of FRENICHES (N.8.d.b) Batteries were withdrawn to positions in U.15 and V.16 at Fme. du FONDS GOYERS in support of 62nd French Division.	
BEAULIEU	25/3/18	12.10 am	The enemy himself embarrassed to ERENCOU (O.27) He hour ham withdrawn & positions S. of in square U.19.d. immediately west of BEAULIEU. Brigade in action at 8 pm H.Q. LA 30 M ESSE F.I.E.	SHEET 70 FRANCE 1:40,000
		1 pm	Batteries withdrawn to position in square T.29.a with HQ at AUBICOURT (T.21)	
AUBICOURT		6 pm		
BALNY FARM	26/3/18	2 am	Batteries ordered to withdraw to positions on B.14.b.b.d. west of CANIZOLI-BOIS-LE-COMTE. Batteries in action at 5.30 am with HQ at BALNY FARM (B.14.d) H.Q. 62nd French Division had given orders to their artillery to retire to rejoin his infantry, but had neglected to tell the British artillery attached to him therefore a husty withdrawal was made and retire was made via FRESNOY & BUSSY.	

Army Form C. 2118.

WAR DIARY
or
INTELLIGENCE SUMMARY.
(Erase heading not required.)

Instructions regarding War Diaries and Intelligence Summaries are contained in F. S. Regs., Part II. and the Staff Manual respectively. Title pages will be prepared in manuscript.

Place	Date	Hour	Summary of Events and Information	Remarks and references to Appendices
GURY	26.3.18	12.30pm	The batteries were forced into an flew spots man Fleant instead our FS	FRANCE
LA GENSE FARM.		9pm.	Batteries came into action at map LA GENSE FARM in N2/2a and 3a, in support of the 77th French Division	SHEET 1/40,000
ST.CLAID FARM	27/3	2.45pm	Batteries came into action near ST. CLAID FARM (M.5)	SHEET 17
-do-	28/3		Quiet day. Batteries in action as above forming to prevent the enemy from opening	FRANCE
			PIEMONT HILL which was attended severe times by the enemy	SHEET 2
-do-	29/3		Quiet day. Harrassing fire carried out by batteries on enemy communications	BEAUVAIS
-do-	30/3	9am	Town held by 53rd & 177th French Divisions attacked by the enemy in forces & were withdrawn to position in squares M.5.b. succeeded in capturing PRESSE-DE-ROYE (G.24g) & La Chateau Park. 13th Battery	
-do-		5.30pm	The French launched a counter attack and took all lost ground. 70th Division	
-do-		9pm	Batteries moved to position E. GRANDFRESNOY (about 8 miles S.W. PIERREPONT(?))	
GRANDFRESNOY	31/3/18	1pm	What was left of 25, 30th & 311 Batteries moved to LA NEUVILLE over (about 4 miles N.W. of CLERMONT) to LA NEUVILLE. B. NC/153. OA SORTEI(?)	
			D/153. title of FORMAT MARTINVAL	

[signature] Kavanagh
Lieut. Col RFA
2I/C

for (Commanding) CLXIII Brigade RFA

36th Divisional Artillery.

153rd BRIGADE R.F.A. ::: APRIL 1918.

Army Form C. 2118.

WAR DIARY
or
INTELLIGENCE SUMMARY.
(Erase heading not required.)

153rd Brigade R.F.A.
April 1918.

Place	Date	Hour	Summary of Events and Information	Remarks and references to Appendices
WARIVILLE & LORTIET	1/4/18		Brigade resting in billets. Cleaning up.	Sheet BEAUVAIS 1:100,000. AMIENS 1:100,000. DIEPPE 1:100,000
FRANCASTEL	2/4/18		Brigade marched to Francastel and rested for the night.	
MORVILLERS ST. SATURNIN	3/4/18		Brigade marched to Morvillers-St. Saturnin.	
ditto	4/4/18 to 7/4/18		Brigade being refitted by G.O.C. Poix Collecting Area.	
MOYENCOURT SOUS POIX	8/4/18		Brigade marched to Moyencourt-Sous-Poix.	AMIENS 1:100,000
ditto	9/4/18 to 10/4/18		Brigade resting.	
RENANCOURT par AMIENS	11/4/18		Brigade marched to Renancourt.	
ditto	12/4/18 & 13/4/18		Brigade resting and waiting to entrain.	

WAR DIARY
INTELLIGENCE SUMMARY

153rd Brigade R.F.A.

April 1918 (Cont)

Army Form C. 2118.

Place	Date	Hour	Summary of Events and Information	Remarks and references to Appendices
AMIENS	14/4/18		Brigade entrained at St. Roch Station, Amiens.	Sheet AMIENS 1:100,000
POPERINGHE	15/4/18		Brigade detrained at Hopoutre Siding, Poperinghe, and bivouacked near Godewaersvelde	
BERTHEN	16/4/18		The Brigade came into action near Berthen in support of the 34th Divisional Infantry. H.Q. at SPOTTERKE (R.15.d.1030) batteries located as follows:- A/153. R.21.a.9050 B/153. R.22.a.1050 C/153. R.21.b.8020 D/153. R.21.b.2040 Harassing fire was opened as soon as batteries were ready to fire, on to BAILLEUL and the AERODROME and continued throughout the night. At about 7.20 a.m. the enemy essayed to break through our lines opposite BAILLEUL but our barrage effectively checked any advance on his part. H.Q. moved at 10 a.m. back to R.114.b.6060. O.P.s were established on MONT NOIR, R.15.a.8020 and R.20.c logo.	Sheet 27 1:40,000
	17/4/18		Harassing fire was maintained at rate of 60 rounds per battery per hour.	

WAR DIARY
INTELLIGENCE SUMMARY

153rd Brigade R.F.A.

April 1918 (Cont.)

Army Form C. 2118.

Place	Date	Hour	Summary of Events and Information	Remarks and references to Appendices
BERTHEN	18/4/18		Nothing of importance occurred this day, the same rate of harassing fire being continued. Hostile aircraft were active over our lines.	Sheet 27 1:40,000
	19/4/18		A prisoner captured during the night gave information that the AERODROME at Boilleul was much used by troops in reserve. Fire was therefore directed on to this spot.	
	20/4/18		Quiet day. Nothing of importance occurred.	
	21/4/18		BAILLEUL is in flames owing to our shelling. Hostile artillery was very active in the battery and back areas.	
	22/4/18		Day quiet. Usual harassing fire continued. Batteries withdrew to wagon lines at Godewaersvelde.	
HAMHOEK	23/4/18		Brigade marched to HAMHOEK and came under 36th Division.	
	24/4/18		Resting.	
	25/4/18		Brigade moved to BRIEKEN and 1 section for battery relieved 1 section of 66th Divisional Artillery covering 36th Divisional Infantry, as follows:- H.Q. Canal Bank C.25.d.10.70. A/153. B.30.d.30.70. B/153. B.30.b.00.60. C/153. C.26.a.80.30. D/153. C.25.c.70.90.	

WAR DIARY or INTELLIGENCE SUMMARY

153rd Brigade R.F.A.
April 1918 (Cont.)

Army Form C. 2118.

Place	Date	Hour	Summary of Events and Information	Remarks and references to Appendices
YPRES	26/4/18		Remaining sections of batteries came into action and owing to infantry withdrawing to a line west of Steenbeck to take Reserve Trench batteries came into action complete as follows:-	Sheet 27 1:40.000
			A/153. B.30.d.30%.	
			B/153. B.30.b.00.80.(4guns) C.25.c.80.80 (2guns)	
			C/153. B.28.d.86.60.	
			D/153. C.25.c.70.90.	
			A brisk harassing fire was maintained throughout the period on all enemy tracks, roads and likely places of assembly.	
	27/4/18		D/153 Battery fired 350 rounds on RAT FARM and BOSSAERT FARM during the day. Harassing fire was kept up during the whole day and night. O.P's established at PICKIEHAYSE No. C.23.c.60.80	
	28/4/18		Harassing fire maintained as usual and counter-preparation fired from 5pm - 5.55pm. on all enemy approaches & likely places of assembly.	
	29/4/18		Counter-preparations fired from 4.30am to 5.15am and 6.45pm to 7.30pm and harassing fire continued. Concentrations were fired on RAT FARM and BOSSAERT FARM. Hostile artillery were slightly more active during the day near WIELTJE.	

Army Form C. 2118.

153rd Brigade R.F.A.
April 1918 (Cont)

WAR DIARY
or
INTELLIGENCE SUMMARY

(Erase heading not required.)

Instructions regarding War Diaries and Intelligence Summaries are contained in F. S. Regs., Part II. and the Staff Manual respectively. Title pages will be prepared in manuscript.

Place	Date	Hour	Summary of Events and Information	Remarks and references to Appendices
YPRES	30/4/18		Counter-preparation was fired from 3.30am to 4.20am & 6.30pm to 7.20pm. Concentrations were fired during the night on all "Pill-boxes and farms known to be occupied by the enemy. A brisk harassing fire was maintained on enemy communications throughout the period.	Sheet 27 1.40.0.00

C.H. Sotts
Lieut Col R.F.A.
Commanding 153rd Brigade R.F.A.

7/5/18.

Army Form C. 2118.

WAR DIARY
or
INTELLIGENCE SUMMARY.
(Erase heading not required.)

Instructions regarding War Diaries and Intelligence Summaries are contained in F.S. Regs., Part II. and the Staff Manual respectively. Title pages will be prepared in manuscript.

153rd Brigade R.F.A.

May 1918.

Vol 24

Place	Date	Hour	Summary of Events and Information	Remarks and references to Appendices
YPRES	1st.		Harassing fire carried out during the 24 hours on selected targets. An enemy 77 mm Battery was located True bearing 580° from PICKELHAUBE HOUSE.	
	2nd.		Counter Preparation was carried out in the early hours of the morning on likely places of assembly. Harassing fire, calibration and registration carried out by Batteries. A new trench is reported being dug from UHLAN FARM to approx. C.29.b.70.00. Machine Gun active from JASPER FARM during night 2/3rd.	
	3rd.		Counter Preparation carried out in early hours of morning on likely places of assembly. Harassing fire and calibration continued. Enemy L.Gs active against our aircraft during afternoon. The ST.JULIEN-ZONNEBEKE Road is always used by the enemy towards dusk - ration parties and transport being seen. At about 6.0 pm one of our R.E.8 aeroplanes dropped 4 bombs in our lines near PICKELHAUBE and then flew back over our lines.	
	4th.		Counter Preparation carried out in early hours of the morning. Harassing fire continued throughout 24 hours. Concentrations fired on selected targets. At 11.0 pm S.O.S. Signal sent up on the left of the Divl. Front and repeated from ENGLISH FARM. Batteries opened fire on their S.O.S. Lines, but at 11.30 pm Infantry reported all quiet and fire was stopped.	
	5th.		Counter Preparation carried out at 9.15 pm 4/5/18 and 3.40 am 5/5/18. Harassing fire continued throughout 24 hours. Some new work is observed at about C.23.d.5.4. and a T.M. emplacement is suspected. Signalling Lamp was working for 30 seconds from WURST FARM at 5.30 pm.	
	6th.		Harassing fire carried out. Concentrations fired on selected targets. Enemy gun flashes reported on T.B. 830 from HASLER HOUSE.	
	7th.		Harassing fire carried out on all targets likely to annoy the enemy. Enemy M.G. firing from BRIDGE HOUSE. Two periscopes were in use yesterday on the N.W. corner of CHEDDAR VILLA.	
	8th.		Harassing fire carried out during 24 hours. At about 11 am an enemy Bi-plane of a new design flew low over out forward system for about ½ hour.	

Army Form C. 2118.

WAR DIARY
or
INTELLIGENCE SUMMARY.
(Erase heading not required.)

Instructions regarding War Diaries and Intelligence Summaries are contained in F. S. Regs., Part II. and the Staff Manual respectively. Title pages will be prepared in manuscript.

Place	Date	Hour	Summary of Events and Information	Remarks and references to Appendices
In the Field YPRES	9th.		Harassing fire carried out throughout 24 hours. Much movement observed during day at VEMRULE FARM.	
	10th.		Harassing fire carried out on Tracks and selected targets. Occasional movement observed round FARMS on HILL 35.	
	11th.		Harassing fire continued. Concentration was fired at 12 noon from U.29.c.33.79. - 46.50.	
	12th.		Concentration fired at 12 noon in co-operation with Heavy Artillery on C.24.c.87.06. - C.30.a.90.90. Nineteen enemy balloons visible from one battery position at 7.0 pm.	
	13th.		A formation of ten hostile aeroplanes flew over battery area at 9.15 am, one flying very low, the whole formation flying at about 2000 ft. 18 enemy balloons visible from one battery position from daybreak until about 9.45 am. Harassing fire continued.	
	14th.		Counter Preparation was fired from 3.5 am - 4.0 am on likely places of assembly. Enemy aircraft very active throughout day.	
	15th.		Harassing fire and calibration carried out on Pill-Boxes tracks, and centres of activity. Gas concentrations were fired during night 15/16th May. A visual station is suspected at VERLORENHOEK. Fires seen in the enemys lines during the day.	
	16th.		Gas concentrations fired during night 16/17th May. Enemy Aircraft active during day.	
	17th.		Counter Preparation carried out during night 17/18th May, on likely places of assembly. Concentrations were carried out on selected targets, and an enemy ammunition dump set on fire. Much movement observed during the day in the enemy lines.	
	18th.		Harassing fire continued. Gas concentrations were fired during the night 18/19th May. Enemy bombing machines active during night.	
	19th.		Harassing fire, and Group Concentrations carried out on places likely to annoy the enemy. Enemy balloon brought down by our planes at a hearing of 289 from POTIJZE BAR O.P. at 9.45 am. At 8 pm one of our balloons brought down by enemy plane.	

Army Form C. 2118.

WAR DIARY
or
INTELLIGENCE SUMMARY.
(Erase heading not required.)

Instructions regarding War Diaries and Intelligence Summaries are contained in F.S. Regs., Part II. and the Staff Manual respectively. Title pages will be prepared in manuscript.

Place	Date	Hour	Summary of Events and Information	Remarks and references to Appendices
YPRES.	20th.		Harassing fire continued. Gas concentration fired on crossing of STEENBEKE C.19.c.25.15. Trench Mortars active, at C.29.c.8.5. A dump at ODER HOUSE was set on fire by 4.5" Hows. Enemy aircraft active in morning and evening.	
	21st.		Harassing fire continued. Gas concentrations were fired during the night 21/22nd on Crossing of STEENBEKE and BRIDGE HOUSE. Gun flashes observed on bearings of 51° & 39° from HATLER HOUSE.	
	22nd.		Harassing fire carried out. Much movement observed in enemy's lines.	
	23rd.		Concentrations fired on selected targets. Very little aerial activity.	
	24th.		Harassing fire continued. Enemy T.M. active at C.29.c.61.59.	
	26th.		Concentrations fired during night on selected targets to annoy the enemy. Harassing fire continued.	
	27th.		Enemy aircraft more active. Retaliatory fire was brought to bear on OUTPOST BUILDINGS, UHLAN FARM, and GREY RUIN.	
	28th.		Hostile aircraft very active during morning and evening. Harassing fire continued.	
	29th.		Hostile aircraft active in early morning. Several balloons were visible from HATLER HOUSE. Harassing fire carried out in co-operation with H.A.	
	30th.		Gas concentration fired at 3.45 am on C.18.d.28.38. Harassing fire and Group concentrations carried out on selected targets. A detached section in C.19.d. heavily shelled during morning. Enemy aircraft active. Several balloons were visible. (At 8.15 pm 5 of our balloons were brought down by Enemy Aircraft. 29/5/18) *[handwritten annotations]*	
	31st.		Harassing fire continued. Concentrations fired on selected targets. E.A. active. Concentrations fired during night on selected targets.	

Lt. Col. R.F.A.
Commanding 159rd Bde. R.F.A.

Army Form C. 2118.

WAR DIARY
INTELLIGENCE SUMMARY.
(Erase heading not required.)

153rd Brigade R.F.A.

June 1918.

Place	Date	Hour	Summary of Events and Information	Remarks and references to Appendices
In the field	June 1st		Harassing fire carried out on tracks and selected targets. Enemy barrage very active during forenoon. 3 planes flying low are fairly frequent also driven off by our A.A. and M.G. fire. Enemy bombing machines very active during night over back area.	
	June 2nd		Harassing fire continued. Weather conditions unfavourable for aircraft. Night quiet.	
	June 3rd		Harassing fire continued. 9 holes followed targets. Enemy guns are battery position from day trench line about 10am. About 2pm a Jerusalem of 6 enemy planes unaccompanied attacked 4 of our observation balloons. Three enemy planes engaged one of our balloons. Planes withdrew. Results night quiet.	
	June 4th		Harassing fire and group concentrations carried out on areas likely to harass the enemy. Occasional movement forced round Dinepple on three 3.5 Aircraft noise during day. 5 enemy bombing machines were again active over back area.	
	June 5		Commencement of relief of Divisional Artillery by 12th Belgian	

Army Form C. 2118.

WAR DIARY
or
INTELLIGENCE SUMMARY.
(Erase heading not required.)

153rd Brigade R.F.A.

June 1915.

Place	Date	Hour	Summary of Events and Information	Remarks and references to Appendices
Field (continued)	June 6th		Devries. One Section of each battery relieves during night. Harassing fire and troop concentrations on roads, tracks, Railway and Valley assembly places. Enemy averages fairly active during the morning. Shelling of track near causeway above Dromore. Relief continued after Anti-Aircraft Section of each battery being relieved.	
	June 7th		Day comparatively quiet. Relief of Brigade completed by Kinneys Bde. remaining Sections attached to Kinneys Brigade moved from Wagon lines on Tuesdays to Campigny Wood Halfway 6.10.C.23. A/153 6.17.6.0.9. B/153 I.16.a.9.4. Post W.O.S.1. A/153 I.16.a.9.4.	
	June 9th		Inspection of Brigade by Second Army Commander.	
	June 10th & 11th June 5th		Section gunnery carries out	
	June 11th June 21st		Battery training.	
	June 22nd		Brigade sports	
	June 23rd & June 30th		Battery training continues Inspection of horses by R.F.R.A. II Corps.	

Bird Loa Lt Col.
Commanding 153rd Brigade R.F.A.

153rd BRIGADE R.F.A.   WAR DIARY

INTELLIGENCE SUMMARY.

(Erase heading not required.)

Army Form C. 2118.

July 1918.

Instructions regarding War Diaries and Intelligence Summaries are contained in F. S. Regs., Part II. and the Staff Manual respectively. Title pages will be prepared in manuscript.

Place	Date	Hour	Summary of Events and Information	Remarks and references to Appendices
HANDEKOT.	1st		36th Divisional Horse Show held at PROVEN AERODROME (F.13.b.) No. training carried out.	All map reference Sheet 27 BELGIUM & Part of FRANCE.
	2nd.		Battery training resumed.	
	3rd.		Battery training carried out in the morning. 36th Divisional Artillery Sports held at E.16.d.80.80. in the afternoon. Enemy bombing planes were active over our back areas during the night.	
	4th		The Brigade marched from the HANDEKOT Divisional Artillery Area via WATOU; WINNEZEELE (J.17.a.) RWELD (J.27.) to billets in and near HARDIFORT (I.30.a.) with Brigade H.Q. at the MAIRE, HARDIFORT.	
HARDIFORT.	5th		The Brigade Commander reconnoitred positions being taken over from the 4th Field Artillery Regiment.	Appendix "A" attached.
BERTHEN.	6th		Batteries went into action as follows:-	
			A/153 Battery R.F.A. 4 guns. R.29.d.08.92.	
			B/153 Battery R.F.A. 4 guns. R.23.c.70.30.	
			C/153 Battery R.F.A. 2 guns. R.22.d.10.92.	
			D/153 Battery R.F.A. 4 guns. R.24.c.80.81.	
	7th		Remaining guns came into action as follows:-	
			A/153 Battery R.F.A. 2 guns. R.29.c.05.90.	
			B/153 Battery R.F.A. 2 guns. R.29.a.10.40.	
			C/153 Battery R.F.A. 2 guns. R.22.d.10.92.	
			D/153 Battery R.F.A. 2 guns. M.19.d.71.87.	
	8th		H.Q. established at CATO COPSE in R.16.d. taking over from the 4th French Field Artillery Regt. The following O.Ps were taken over from the French and manned.	Left Group Order No. 1 attached.
			(1) ERNEST O.P. M.28.a.95.95. (manned as rocket guard by night & Group O.P. by day).	
			(2) PIERRE O.P. R.16.d.80.40. (manned as Group O.P. by day only).	
			408 & 409 Batteries (96th Army Field Artillery Brigade) in positions as under came under the orders of this Brigade and with the four batteries of 153rd Brigade R.F.A. formed the POTTER GROUP.	Appendix "A".
			408 Battery. 4 guns R.27.b.50.35. 2 guns R.21.d.40.05.	
			409 Battery. 4 guns R.28.c.55.85. 2 guns R.28.a.80.05.	
	9th		Wagon Lines of 153rd Brigade R.F.A. established in and near Q.6.d.	
	10th		S.O.S. Lines registered. Harassing fire carried out.	
	11th		Registration and Harassing fire carried out. Harassing fire maintained.	

WAR DIARY
INTELLIGENCE SUMMARY

Place	Date	Hour	Summary of Events and Information	Remarks and references to Appendices
BERTHEN	12th		Registration and Harassing Fire. Much enemy movement seen on BAILLEUL-NIEPPE-ARMENTIERES Road.	
	13th		Registration and harassing fire.	
	14th		Harassing Fire carried out.	
	15th		Harassing fire carried out throughout the day and night on roads, tracks etc. Enemy Artillery showed increased activity.	
	16th		The Group fired in support of a raid by the 12th R.I.R. vide appendix "B" attached. The enterprise was not a success, and no identifications were secured. Batteries moved to main positions as follows from where the BLUE LINE can be effectively covered on the whole Divisional Front. A/153 Battery R.F.A. R.17.a.20.63. (4 guns) B/153 Battery R.F.A. R.16.b.70.21. (4 guns) 408 Battery R.F.A. R.16.a.20.50. (4 guns) 409 Battery R.F.A. R.17.d.40.88. (4 guns)	
	17th		The 410 Battery R.F.A. came under orders of POTTER GROUP and brought 4 guns in action at R.17.d.15.65.	
	18th		Counter Preparation was carried out in accordance with Appendix "C" attached. Detached sections moved to locations as follows:- A/153 Battery R.F.A. R.17.a.15.15. B/153 Battery R.F.A. R.17.a.30.10. 408 Battery R.F.A. R.16.a.40.80. 409 Battery R.F.A. R.17.c.85.25.	Appendix "D" attached.
	19th	7.55 am	Remaining guns of 410 Battery R.F.A. came into action at R.17.d.15.65. 409 & D/153 Batteries fired in support of an attack on METEREN by the 9th Division in accordance with appendix "E" attached. For this purpose 408 Battery was lent to SIMPSON GROUP and fired a barrage from its old position at R.27.b.50.35. D/173 was lent to POTTER GROUP for this operation.	
	20th		Harassing fire on selected targets carried out. T.Ms S.9.c.2.0.; S.9.b.88.40.; S.8.d.90.50.; S.9.c.88.40.; S.9.c.10.00.; S.9.c.30.50.; S.9.c.20.00.; and M.G. at S.9.c.60.83.	
	21st		The Group fired in support of a raid by the 9th R. Innis. Fusrs. on enemy posts in square S.8.a. in accordance with appendix "F" attached. This raid resulted in the capture of one prisoner and 2 Machine Guns.	
	22nd		Harassing fire was carried out on selected targets.	
	23rd		Carried out normal harassing fire.	
	24th		Usual harassing fire.	

Army Form C. 2118.

(3)
WAR DIARY
INTELLIGENCE SUMMARY.
(Erase heading not required.)

Instructions regarding War Diaries and Intelligence Summaries are contained in F. S. Regs., Part II. and the Staff Manual respectively. Title pages will be prepared in manuscript.

Place	Date	Hour	Summary of Events and Information	Remarks and references to Appendices
BERTHEN.	25th		The following moves of detached sections took place. 408 Battery R.F.A. to R.21.d.40.05. C/153 & 410 Batteries put out detached sections at R.21.d.95.31. and R.28.c.55.85. Normal harassing fire programme.	
	26th		Usual harassing fire. Enemy's Artillery showed marked increase in activity, our Battery areas being subjected to heavy shelling without, however, any serious damage being done.	
	27th		Usual harassing fire programme. Enemy's Artillery still fairly active in our Battery areas.	
	28th		Gas concentration was fired by this Group in accordance with appendix "G" attached. Decrease in hostile shelling during the day, but at night roads and tracks vigourously harassed.	
	29th		Usual harassing fire. Enemy fire quiet during the day, but active on approaches during the later part of the night.	
	30th		Harassing fire carried out. At 10.0 pm a Group Concentration was fired on "SAUERKRAUT" (see appendix "H" attached). A gas concentration was fired on an hostile Battery position at 10.15 pm at S.21.a.35.55. - S.21.a.30.50. (Appendix "J" attached).	
	31st		Harassing fire maintained by day and night on enemy approaches and tender points. Concentration "RUPPRECHT" was fired at 9.27 pm. Visibility good all day. Enemy Artillery slightly active between dusk and dawn on our approaches.	

Lieut. Col. R.F.A.
Commanding 153rd Brigade R.F.A.

Army Form C. 2118.

WAR DIARY
INTELLIGENCE SUMMARY

153rd Brigade R.F.A.

August 1918.

Instructions regarding War Diaries and Intelligence Summaries are contained in F.S. Regs, Part II. and the Staff Manual respectively. Title pages will be prepared in manuscript.

(Erase heading not required.)

Place	Date	Hour	Summary of Events and Information	Remarks and references to Appendices
BERTHEN.	1st	8.45	pm. Concentration "WILLIAM" fired. 7.31 pm, N.F. call answered, target S.12.d.2.5. 11.20 pm Enemy transport engaged. Usual harassing fire engaged maintained. 10.30 pm Gas concentration on enemy billets S.14.c.98.44.	
	2nd.		2.15 am Gas concentration fired on enemy billets in S.14.c.98.44. 10.25 pm Group concentration "RUPPRECHT" fired. Usual harassing fire. Hostile Artillery has been unusually quiet.	
	3rd.		Harassing fire carried out day and night. 10.0 pm Group concentration "HINDENBERG" fired.	
	4th.		Harassing fire on roads and occupied areas. Group concentration "WILLIAM" fired at 10.0 pm.	
	5th.		Harassing fire.	
	6th.		Concentration "SAUERKRAUT" fired by all Batteries in the Group at 9.40 pm. Usual harassing fire.	
	7th.		9.43 pm. Concentration "PROSIT" fired. Harassing fire carried out. 9.30 pm D/153 in conjunction with other 4.5" Batteries in the Division fired a gas concentration of two minutes duration, the target being the centre of the square in BAILLEUL at S.13.d.55.00.	
	8th.		Harassing fire on selected targets. 7.40 pm N.F. call answered. S.Z.13 (S.23.d.32.50.- 19.46.) 9.45 pm. Group concentration "WILLIAM" fired. Hostile Artillery active in our Battery areas.	
	9th.		Harassing fire carried out. 9.3 pm. Group concentration "HINDENBERG" fired. 12 midnight A.B.C.D. 153rd Bde. and 408 Battery fired in support of gas projector attack.	
	10th.		Usual harassing fire. 10.3 pm Gas concentration on S.14.d.55.82. 8.40 pm N.F. call answered.	
	11th.		Usual harassing fire carried out. 9.5 pm Concentration "SAUERKRAUT" fired.	
	12th.		Harassing fire carried out. Concentration "PROSIT" fired at 9.45 pm. Hostile Artillery exceptionally quiet.	
	13th.		1.30 am The Group co-operated with the 2nd and 99th Brigades R.G.A. who fired a concentration on Support Companys billets in BAILLEUL. 3.0 pm Bombardment of enemy post at S.7.d.45.50, with	

Army Form C. 2118.

WAR DIARY
INTELLIGENCE SUMMARY

(Erase heading not required.)

Instructions regarding War Diaries and Intelligence Summaries are contained in F.S. Regs., Part II. and the Staff Manual respectively. Title pages will be prepared in manuscript.

Place	Date	Hour	Summary of Events and Information	Remarks and references to Appendices
BERTHEN	13th		Incendiary shell. All 18-pdr detached sections fired 15 rounds. 9.15 pm Group concentration "HINDENBERG" fired.	
	14th		Group concentration fired at 9.20 pm, "LUDENDORFF". Usual harassing fire.	
	15th		Group concentration "WILLIAM" fired at 9.15 pm. Usual harassing fire carried out.	
	16th		Group concentration "PROSIT" fired at 9.41 pm. Wire cutting shoot.	9/6 - (2)
	17th		Harassing fire carried out. 9.12 pm Group concentration "LUDENDORFF" fired. Concentration "HINDENBERG" fired at 4.25 am and 4.35 am as punishment for hostile concentration on our left Battalion trenches.	
	18th		Smoke barrage fired in support of operation carried out by Division on our right. This operation was entirely successful. N.F. call answered, NE SZ 2 (S.22.d.3.8.). Usual harassing fire. Group concentration "SAUERKRAUT" fired at 9.15 pm.	9/6 - (3)
	19th		Group concentration "SAUERKRAUT" fired at 11.0 pm. Usual harassing fire carried out.	
	20th		In response to request of Infantry, the following Group Concentrations were fired - 4.55 am. "LUDENDORF", 5.0 am and 5.5 am "RUPPRECHT", 5.45 am "HINDENBERG", 11.58 pm "HINDENBERG". Barrage fired in support of operation carried out by left Division. Operation entirely successful.	
	21st		10.52 pm, S.O.S. fired in support of left Division. Usual harassing fire.	
	22nd		12.30 am, Barrage of 85 minutes duration fired in support of operation carried out by this Division. 4.45 am, S.O.S. fired in support of left Division. Harassing fire carried out. 11.6 am "Help MURAL" fired on until 11.12, when in response to S.O.S. signal on our Group front the normal S.O.S. lines were fired on. 11.27 S.O.S. repeated. 11.46 "stop" from Infantry (Right Battn).	9/6/7, 6/6/13 (4)
	23rd		Wire cutting bombardment carried out. Usual harassing fire carried out.	9/6/7 (5)

Army Form C. 2118.

WAR DIARY
INTELLIGENCE SUMMARY.
(Erase heading not required.)

Place	Date	Hour	Summary of Events and Information	Remarks and references to Appendices
BERTHEN	24th		S.O.S. fired in support of Division on our left at 1.15 am. Harassing fire on roads and occupied areas carried out. 7.0 am - 9.30 am Barrage fired in conjunction with operation by our Infantry. Enemy movement engaged at various times during the morning. Enemy reported to be forming up for counter attack in S.9.a. at 2.40 pm, engaged by Batteries of this Group. During the afternoon and early evening movement in BAILLEUL engaged. 7.35 - 8.33 pm, barrage put down on protective barrage lines to stop counter attack made by by enemy. 10.30, 10.40. and 10.50. pm counter preparations fired, batteries searching forward from 200x - 500x beyond normal S.O.S.	
	25th.		4.20. 4.35, & 4.40 am, concentrations fired.	
	26th.		Concentration "RUPPRECHT" fired at 4.45 pm. Harassing fire carried out during night.	
	27th.		10.30 pm, Group concentration fired on target 48. 10.48 pm N.F.call answered target X.X S.Z.21. 6.25 pm N.F. call answered target S.Z.1. Harassing fire carried out during the night.	
	28th.		Concentration fired on target No. 13. Harassing fire carried out during night.	
	29th.		Usual harassing fire carried out. During the day a large number of fires were observed in enemy lines suggestive of a withdrawal. At night fires blazed in enemy lines from ESTAIRES to ARMENTIERES. Our line was not advanced during the night.	
	30th.		D/153 fired on the road from S.16.c. to S.17.d. on enemy M.Gs. During the day our patrols felt their way forward and at 9.0 pm Infantry Left Battalion line were holding positions as follows during night - from S.10.c.05.25. to S.11.a.75.35. Batteries advanced to positions as follows during night - A/153 4 guns to M.25.d.10.90., B/153 6 guns to R.30.c.45.70., C/153 6 guns to M.31.b.45.60., D/153 4 guns to M.25.d.10.27. (detached section left at M.19.d.90.76.), 409 Bty 6 guns to M.26.c.00.65., 410 Bty 6 guns to M.26.c.60.80. One section from A/153 went forward under 2nd Lt. K.A.McMILLAN at dusk to report to Infantry Battalion Commander at TRESCOTT HOUSE (S.3.d.30.70.) with instructions to come into action against enemy machine guns on the Ravelsberg.	
	31st.		Batteries advanced during the afternoon and evening to positions in S.9.d. and S.10. b & c. Our Infantry continue to work forward. Our Infantry take KEMMEL HILL and the Ravelsberg	

Army Form C. 2118.

WAR DIARY
(4)
INTELLIGENCE SUMMARY.
(Erase heading not required.)

Instructions regarding War Diaries and Intelligence Summaries are contained in F. S. Regs., Part II. and the Staff Manual respectively. Title pages will be prepared in manuscript.

Place	Date	Hour	Summary of Events and Information	Remarks and references to Appendices
BERTHEN	1st		during the morning without opposition. 6.50 pm, the section of A/153 was ordered to rejoin the main position at approximately S.10.c.40.70. Batteries in action as follows:- A/153 S.10.c.50.70.; B/153 S.15.b.90.90.; C/153 S.10.b.00.90.; D/153 S.M 4.d.00.60.; 409 S.9.b.50.30.; 410 S.10.c.30.50., with centre line of fire on T.20.central. C/153 relieved 409 Bty at Left Liaison. At night each Battery fired 50 rounds harassing fire on squares T.20.c., T.26., and B.2. Line runs S.29.central. S.22.d.0.6., S.23.b.5.7.	

Lieut. Col. R.F.A.
Commanding 153rd Brigade R.F.A.

Army Form C. 2118.

WAR DIARY
INTELLIGENCE SUMMARY:
(Erase heading not required.)

153rd Brigade R.F.A.

September 1918.

Place	Date	Hour	Summary of Events and Information	Remarks and references to Appendices
Neuve Eglise	11/9/18 to 17/9/18		All Batteries in action in support of Infantry attacking and capturing NEUVE EGLISE	
	18/9/18		At dawn enemy Batteries pulled out and went to them respective wagon lines. B/153 Bde R.F.A. and 153 Bde R.F.A. took over command of the front	
Croix De Poperinghe	19/9/18		Batteries remained at their wagon lines in the CROIX DE POPERINGHE area. No Section affiliation to the Brigade	
	20/9/18		The Brigade and Hqrs Section DAC moved at night to the HAAN DE KOT area near SCHREXEN - BERTHEN - ABEELE - WATOU.	
Haan de Kot	21/9/18		Positions of Batteries was as follows: H.Q. E.11.c.0.y PENSHURST CAMP B/153 E.10.d.5.8. RUNSTEAD CAMP B/153 E.10.6.4.8 PLURENDEN CAMP C/153 E.11.a.8.6 PEONI CAMP D/153 E.21.6.8.8 POPPLETON CAMP Hqr Sec. D.A.C. E.17.c.6.8.	
	22/9/18		Enemy positions in outskirts of YPRES reconnoitred Brigade to move attached to 9th Division.	
	28/9/18		Batty of 10ffrs and 12 men for Battery go up to take over Battery	

Army Form C. 2118.

WAR DIARY
INTELLIGENCE SUMMARY.
(Erase heading not required.)

September 1918   (153 Brigade R.F.A.)

Place	Date	Hour	Summary of Events and Information	Remarks and references to Appendices
HONDEKOT	24/9/18 (contd)		Positions, wagon lines thrown in A 28 d.	
"	25/9/18		Stationary.	
"	26/9/18		Stationary.	
"	27/9/18		Brigade marched to the Canter Genies hules in A 28 d. the guns went up into action but only "C" Battery guns were left. Road runs via WATOU - ST JANTER BIZEN & POPERINGHE	
A 28 d	28/9/18		Brigade Headquarters moved to its advanced headquarters in the RAMPARTS YPRES in the evening the detachments etc joined their Battery in the advanced positions. The Brigade to covering the 28th Infantry Brigade	
RAMPARTS	28/9/18		Infantry. The 9th Division in conjunction with Belgians on the left and other Divisions on the right will attack the enemy, the objective of the division being the ridge from south edge of the Polygone de ZONNEBEKE to D.19.a.30.20. In the attack successes to advance Battle order. BERCELAERE 28th Infantry Brigade on right. 28 Infantry Brigade on left. 27 Infantry Brigade in Reserve from SOLVA 242 Belgian Connected on 3 Kms filamen Tuentrances Pr.2920 on the relation on Kero-S (St.Jean) on enemy resistance. In YPRES was slightly the open almost unnecessary enemy range engage unwilling range was confined particularly to gun line Thereof recovers and F.O.O. in POTIJE 6 won enemy inconsisting the helly "On Infantry from the close killed on front Advanced reports to the enemy offering no resistance confirming and the advance continuing weekend at Westhoek receive from Brigade Major

Army Form C. 2118.

WAR DIARY
or
INTELLIGENCE SUMMARY.

(Erase heading not required.)

September 1918.

Place	Date	Hour	Summary of Events and Information	Remarks and references to Appendices
RAMPARTS	20/9/18 (Cont)	9.0 p.m.	Report that at 6.40 a.m. one Infantry were seen crawling from BROODSEINDE Cross Roads. Message from POLYGON BUTT. 200 Prisoners taken at POLYGON CRUCIFIX. Enemy opposite POLYGON CRUCIFIX 12-15 reported to any Front Bns. were suffered to have the men rest at the CAMBRIDGE ROAD line the one DCBA were in support to Black one form to CAMBRIDGE RD A coy B Black on the front stay till evening and then were very far in advance of the enemy we moved up to POTIJZE very few by the time Enemy reached GHELUVELT. Very heavy Fire from FREZENBERG. There was one big gun opposite the SHOTEHOFFE. One was noted to move on from of fire just on CALL RIDGE. This was done by barrage during the attack. We were not in action till in afternoon for Gas was sent to BECELAERE. We held at night on D25 C Central with SMITH BECELAERE Ridge the road on right inclosive to a Crossroads with MISSION SAELE. Road of the Pepper Canister to one road right bit by G.25 B in the tenth of influence ... Canister to one	
D.2.5.c 6.15 a.m.	29/9/18		As very 9 p.m. 2/3rd had got Rifle 10/He Grenades at 1/Cons .... altered to reconoitre positions this Brigade to be relieved by .... KRS (TERHAND) and .... on left. (3rd) R.B. on right (3rd Bde of Brigade)	
....	30/9/18		....	

Army Form C. 2118.

WAR DIARY
or
INTELLIGENCE SUMMARY.
(Erase heading not required.)

September 1918   153rd Bde R.F.A.

Instructions regarding War Diaries and Intelligence Summaries are contained in F. S. Regs, Part II. and the Staff Manual respectively. Title pages will be prepared in manuscript.

Place	Date	Hour	Summary of Events and Information	Remarks and references to Appendices
K.16.b.57	30/9/18 (contd)	9.30pm	he is reported to have retaken there up by two named Commanders there and two days and movement has been extremely difficult	

Signed,
Maj. R.F.A.
Commanding 153rd Brigade R.F.A.

153rd Brigade R.F.A.
Army Form C. 2118.

WAR DIARY
or
INTELLIGENCE SUMMARY.
(Erase heading not required.)

October 1918.

Vol 34

Instructions regarding War Diaries and Intelligence Summaries are contained in F. S. Regs., Part II. and the Staff Manual respectively. Title pages will be prepared in manuscript.

Place	Date	Hour	Summary of Events and Information	Remarks and references to Appendices
	1st		Batteries in action in positions as follows :- A/153. 28/K.21.a.60.80. B/153. K.21.a.65.65. C/153. K.14.b.30.30. D/153. K.15.d.80.60. H.Q. K.14.b.50.10. Barrage fired at 6.15 am in support of attack by 108th Infantry Brigade on Hill 41. Attack successful, but enemy counter attacked at 10 am and retook the Hill. 10.20 am Reported that 108 Inf. Bde. were again in possession. 11.40 am line approximately K.18.d.7.6. - TWIG FARM - K.9.a.0.0. - K.24.central - K.23.b.10.00. - K.26.d.4.0. - K.22.b.6.0. 3.0. pm. At request of G.O.C., 109th Inf. Bde. the following were engaged. Farm L.14.a.4.6., Cross Roads L.14.b.1.5. 109th Inf. Bde. endeavouring to turn Hill 41 from the North via KANDEOHOEK, K.12, LEDEGHEM, and moving south astride LEDEGHEM-MENIN Railway. 3.30 pm. Enemy Infantry reported assembling in MYRTLE FARM L.19.b.3.3. 'arr engaged by B/153 Battery for 10 minutes. 8.30 pm Line reported as follows:- K.29.central - K.29.b.8.2. - K.24.a.4.4. - K.24.b.5.3. K.30.a.2.8. - K.24.c.4.2. - K.23.d.9.9. - along east edge of wood - K.24.a.4.4. - K.24.b.5.3. K.24.b.9.6. - K.19.d.9.0. - L.13.c.5.1. - L.13.d.1.4. - L.13.central - Cross Roads L.1.c.8.1. (107th & 108th Inf. Bdes) In touch with 9th Division who hold LEDEGHEM.	
	2nd.		107th Inf. Bde. in conjunction with 29th Division attacked towards MENIN-ROULERS Railway supported by 173rd Brigade R.F.A. N.F. calls received during the day and answered by D/153 Battery. Ammunition at D.26.a. and D.27. packed upto guns. Wagon Lines near BECELAIRE with forward wagon lines for gun limbers and firing battery wagon teams nearer guns.	
	3rd.		Group O.P. established at K.23.a.4.2. S.O.S. received at 5.5 pm, repeated at 5.16 pm. C/153 Battery pushed forward a section to K.10.c.9.0. under 2nd Lt. J.H. WILLIAMS. Batteries fired on S.O.S. lines until 5.55 pm. 6.2 pm enemy reported breaking through on front of 2nd Innis. Fus. (Left Battn) probably at K.24.a. Battn. H.Q. under rifle fire at BASS FARM. Message from 109th Inf. Bde. that Left Battn. had been attacked along its front and that left had been pushed back. 8.20 pm whole situation restored by counter attack. H.Q. moved to K.15.a.2.4.	

Army Form C. 2118.

WAR DIARY
or
INTELLIGENCE SUMMARY.
(Erase heading not required.)

Place	Date	Hour	Summary of Events and Information	Remarks and references to Appendices
	4th		During night of 3/4th enemy very busy with harassing fire, and on morning of 4th heavy counter preparation was put down. Hostile Batteries and T.Ms reported active were engaged by "A" "B" & "C" Batteries. Positions in K.17.a.& c. were reconnoitred and Batteries commenced dumping ammunition at dusk. 108th Inf. Bde. relieved 109th Inf. Bde. Weather remains very close and wet.	
	5th		During morning wagon lines were shelled and several horses killed in "A" Battery. Normal harassing fire programme carried out, and carriage of ammunition to forward positions continued. About 9.0 pm Brigade H.Q. shelled and the following casualties caused. Lieut. Col. C.F.POTTER, D.S.O. Wounded. Capt. D.R.CARTWRIGHT wounded, afterwards died. 2nd Lt. R.J.DEWAR, wounded, afterwards died. Capt. S.W.B.HAY, R.A.M.C. Killed. 2nd Lt. BOSTOCK-SMITH, R.E.Signals. Killed. Major H.G.COLLINS, M.C., R.F.A. assumed command of the Brigade, with H.Q. for the night at "D" Bty.	
	6th.		Bde. H.Q. moved to "D" Battery as a temporary measure. Situation on front remains unchanged. Enemy Artillery much more active, and harassing fire on forward and back areas greatly increased. Wagon Lines moved back to 28/C.30.d. and I.4.c. Casualties to horses caused by enemy bombs. Infantry advanced their line in L.13.c. and L.19.a. by capture of MAUSARD FARM and HENNESSY HOUSE.	
	7th.		Brigade comes under command of Lt. Col. SIMPSON (173rd Bde. RFA) and becomes a sub group. H.Q. moves to K.9.a.6.1. Night much quieter.	
	8th.		No change in situation.	
	9th.		Post established by Infantry in K.24.d.4.0. Hostile shelling rather less. "B" Battery move to K.16.a.2.9.	
	10th.		No change in position. Enemy Artillery fire on forward areas still continues heavy. During evening two enemy aeroplanes attacked and brought down in flames 3 of our balloons. One of the enemy aeroplanes was chased by three of our machines and crashed to earth bursting into flames.	
	11th.		Batteries of the Brigade co-operated in supporting an attack by 108th Inf. Bde. on GOLDFLAKE FARM, and by 35th Division further on the right. T.Ms also assisting. Zero hour 10 am.	

Army Form C. 2118.

WAR DIARY
or
INTELLIGENCE SUMMARY.
(Erase heading not required.)

Instructions regarding War Diaries and Intelligence Summaries are contained in F. S. Regs., Part II. and the Staff Manual respectively. Title pages will be prepared in manuscript.

Place	Date	Hour	Summary of Events and Information	Remarks and references to Appendices
	11th		Attack successful, and in addition to capturing GOLDFLAKE FARM a post was established on the road at K.24.d.9.6. and one at L.19.c.4.9. at 5.36 the S.O.S. call was received from Liaison Officer with Left Battn. and Batteries opened fire. At 5.52 everything reported quiet, but at 5.56 the S.O.S. was again repeated, this time on the whole of the Divisional front. Firing was recommenced. STOP received from Liaison Officer at 6.32. GOLDFLAKE and MANSARD FRMs were both lost to the enemy in this counter attack. 17 prisoners were captured in attack on GOLDFLAKE and one in the counter attack.	
	12th		Infantry retook MANSARD FARM, but GOLDFLAKE remained in enemy hands. One prisoner captured. One section per battery moved up to new positions in K.17.	
	13th		Infantry attacked and took GOLDFLAKE FARM and one heavy machine gun at 5.0 pm. Usual night harassing fire rather more pronounced. "B" Battery moved their guns forward at 8 p.m. "C" Battery carried out harassing fire from 8.11 p.m. and then moved up. "A" Battery, one gun carried out harassing fire from 11 pm to 1 am, and one gun from 1 am to 3 am, and then moved up. "D" Battery fired with 1 Howr. until 3 a.m. All guns reported in new positions and on S.O.S. Lines safely. Bde. H.Q. moved at 4.0 pm to K.17.d.65.65.	
	14th		The battle is resumed. 'H' hour 5.35 am. At 'H' hour minus 3 minutes our barrage opened very accurately, and was very heavy. The enemy made an immediate reply with a protective barrage which caused a considerable number of casualties to our Infantry. BASS FARM and neighbourhood came in for a good deal of shelling - some gas being noticeable. "A" Battery moved forward at 'H' plus 100 in support of the 1st Battn. Innis. Fus. Information received at 11.30 am that they were in action supporting the Infantry at L.15.d. Major GUINNESS (C/153) went forward to reconnoitre and reported at 11.0 am that the enemy were 1000 yards beyond MOORSEELE, and M.G. fire could be heard due south from GOLDEN CROSS ROADS, L.22.c. The enemy resistance except at first was apparently very slight, and good progress was being made. Prisoners seemed to be coming in fairly freely. At 10.40 am report received that the leading Battalion, 1st.R.Innis. Fus. were holding road at L.17.a.9.5. to ELIZABETH RIDGE and had been held up at 8.55 am at SACK MILL. Battn. H.Q. were established in NELLIBARGAIN FARM. Rifle fire sounding very close here. Prisoners had been taken N. of MOORSEELE. 15th R.I.R. reported E. of MOORSEELE at 10.30 am and doing well. Orders were received that forward positions were to be reconnoitred in K.18.d., K.24.b., and L.13.c. from R.A.H.Q. and "B" Battery moved forward and took up a position at K.24.a.8.7. at 10.30 am. "D" Battery also moved forward to L.14.d. No further news of "A"Bty.	

Army Form C. 2118.

WAR DIARY
or
INTELLIGENCE SUMMARY.
(Erase heading not required.)

Instructions regarding War Diaries and Intelligence Summaries are contained in F. S. Regs., Part II. and the Staff Manual respectively. Title pages will be prepared in manuscript.

Place	Date	Hour	Summary of Events and Information	Remarks and references to Appendices
	14th		Meantime the news came through that the situation on the right was favourable, and "C" Battery also moved forward. At 2.0 pm the Brigade Commander moved forward to ASHMORE FARM L.15.c.8.1. with 109th Infantry Brigade H.Q. Bde. H.Q. moved at 3.0 pm and were established by 3.30 pm at L.21.a.17.77. Communication was quickly established with the Batteries in positions as follows. "B" Battery L.11.c.15.08. "C" Battery L.15.d.90.15. "D" Battery L.16.a.4.4. Orders given that 250 rounds per gun had to be dumped and wagons all kept full. Batteries to be ready to fire barrage and move early on morning of 15th. Rear Wagon lines had moved up during day to K.17.central. During "B" & "B" Batteries sustained several casualties to wagon line personnel, many horses being hit. Orders given for "B" "C" & "D" Batteries to carry out harassing fire during night. Four civilians and (including a woman) found in MOORSEELE.	
	15th.		Barrage fired at 9.0 am in support of Infantry attack. "A" Battery moved forward to L.17.a. and were followed by "B" Battery. Orders issued for positions to be reconnoitred in G.9. or G.10. Rear Wagon lines moved to DADIZEELEHOEK xxx. 109th Infantry Bde. at SILVER FARM, L.22.b.4.3. and Div. H.Q. ASHMORE FARM, L.15.c.8.1. Brigade H.Q. moved during afternoon to G.8.d.2.2. and established at 4.15 pm. Batteries were finally in positions as follows. "A" Battery G.15.a.7.5. "B" Battery G.15.a.8.8. "C" Battery G.9.a.7.2. "D" Battery G.9.c.55.40. Orders received later for "A" and "B" Batteries to push on to G.10.d. and positions were occupied as follows. "A" Battery G.10.c.0.2. "B" Battery G.10.c.30.05. Line reported at 10.0 pm approximately as follows - Grid line between G.18. and H.13. G.24.b.5.8., G.23.b.5.0., G.23.d.2.2. Many civilians coming in. Prisoners reported 1 M.O. and 800.R.unwounded and 70 O.R. wounded. Orders in from Divisional Artillery during night. (3.30 am) for barrage at 5.30 am 16th.	
	16th.		Barrage ordered at 5.30 am to support Infantry attack on crossings and bridgehead E. and S.E. of HEULE. 5.20 am orders fro. B.G.R.A. cancelling this. 29th Division reported in COURTRAI "A" Battery moved up to G.17.b.5.5. in support of Infantry followed by "D" Battery. Both Battery Commanders were in close touch with the Infantry and were able to assist by observed shooting on M.Gs and other targets. About 11 am information received from Divisional Artillery that Brigade was to be relieved by 11th A.F.A.Brigade, 41st Division. Two positions occupied by "A" and "B" Batteries would be taken over and two other positions selected by two remaining Batteries. "B" and "C" Batteries not to go forward. Relief of Batteries and H.Q. completed by 5.15 pm. Batteries proceeded to rear wagon lines at DADIZEELEHOEK and afterwards marched to new area F.26 and F.27. via LEDEGHEM. 2nd Lt. D.A.CARSE remained behind as Liaison Officer	

Army Form C. 2118.

WAR DIARY
or
INTELLIGENCE SUMMARY.
(Erase heading not required.)

Place	Date	Hour	Summary of Events and Information	Remarks and references to Appendices
with 108th Infantry Brigade.	16th			
	17th		Day spent resting and cleaning up. Warning order received during evening that Division would proceed next day to relieve 3rd Belgian Division.	
	18th		Brigade Commander and Battery Commanders went forward to reconnoitre positions of readiness in B.18 and B.23. Wagon Lines were reconnoitred and occupied as follows:- H.Q. A.22.b.8.4.; "A" Battery A.23.b.4.2., "B" Battery A.22.d.8.5., "C" Battery B.16.c.5.6., "D" Battery A.22.d.3.0. Orders received at 10 pm that Batteries must move up positions selected and be in position before 9.30 am 19th inst.	
	19th		Batteries in action as follows:- "A" Battery B.18.a.6.1.; "B" Battery B.17.c.25.25.; "C" Battery B.23.a.5.2., "D" Battery B.18.a.7.3. Batteries were silent and no work was done. Bde. H.Q. moved to B.16.b.6.4. Barrage was fired by 18-pdrs and 4.5" Hows. in support of attack to force crossing of the River LYS. Selected points were also bombarded until 2 a.m.	
	20th		2nd Lieut. J.C.FORSTER, C/153, detailed as F.O.O. "C" Battery detailed as Battery to keep in close touch with Infantry. 6.10 am news received that position selected at B.24.b.9.1. 3.45 in action and in touch with 1st R.I.R. covering their advance. Advance of Artillery delayed owing to failure to get bridge across river to take wheeled transport. Footbridge constructed in C.13.30.d., but heavy bridge in C.14. not ready. 9th Division got bridge over at HARLEBEKE, and "D" Battery crossed by this. Reported that Infantry progressing well, and a fair number of prisoners. Locations at 8.0 pm, H.Q. C.25.b.9.5., "A" Battery C.26.c.central, "B" Battery C.19.a.6.3., "C" Battery I.3.a.6.6. with a detached section at I.4.c.9.1. "D" Battery I.3.central.	
	21st		Advance continued without a barrage. Position of Batteries not changed. Very little progress made with bridges. Bde. H.Q. moved to I.3.b.7.6. Later Batteries moved as follows:- "A" Batty. I.1.b.5.7., "B" Battery I.4.c.5.7., "C" Battery I.4.c.9.1., "D" Battery I.3.central. Hostile Artillery fairly active, and M.Gs very active. Infantry advance did not succeed and objectives were not gained. During night 21/22nd "A" and "B" Batteries 173rd Brigade moved up to positions as follows, and were attached to this Brigade. "A" 173rd Bde. I.9.b.4.9. "B" 173rd Bde. I.3.d.4.2.	

Army Form C. 2118.

WAR DIARY
for
INTELLIGENCE SUMMARY.
(Erase heading not required.)

Instructions regarding War Diaries and Intelligence Summaries are contained in F. S. Regs., Part II. and the Staff Manual respectively. Title pages will be prepared in manuscript.

Place	Date	Hour	Summary of Events and Information	Remarks and references to Appendices
	22nd		Advance resumed at 9.0 am with barrage and with covering fire from H.A. (60-pdrs). "C" Battery were shelled while firing barrage with direct aeroplane observation, and some casualties caused. Gas freely used by enemy. At 2.0 pm it was reported that attack on left was held up, and Windmill in J.20 strongly held by enemy. Covering fire was put down by Artillery, and a later report received stated that Infantry had obtained their objectives, and held all the high ground. At 3.0 pm report from 107th Inf. Bde. that Left Coy. was being pushed back, and 18-pdrs and 4.5" Hows opened fire on their protective barrage lines. Fire was maintained on these lines and other specially targets for about two hours, when situation was restored, and Infantry established. "C" Battery moved at 4.0 pm to new position in I.3.c.6.9. Enemy again used gas freely in back area shelling, and 15 cm guns and hows were reported firing. Lieut. Col. C.W.M.IVENS, R.F.A. arrived and assumed command of the Brigade. Warning orders received that barrage would be required on morning of 23rd inst to support attack on left Brigade front.	
	23rd		Information received early that enemy reported retreating on front of Left Brigade and French Infantry pushing on to keep in touch. "B" Battery detailed to accompany leading Battalion. 109th Inf. Bde. relieved 107th Inf. Bde, and established their HQ at I.11.a.7.4. "B" Battery positions were reconnoitred and occupied as follows:- "A" Battery I.17.a.8.4., "B" Battery J.19.b.1.9., "C" Battery I.17.d.9.3., "D" Battery I.17.b.central, H.Q. I.11.d.4.4. Enemy still continues practice of shelling back areas with H.V. 15 cm guns. Bridge over LYS at HARLEBEKE received direct hits and was made impassable for traffic. 3rd Sqdn. 28th Regt. French Dragoons were to push on in front of Infantry and endeavour to seize an old bridge, over SCHELDT between TENHORE and BERCHEM and to capture high ground at KLEINEBORG and BERGHIGK. Later news states held up by M.G. fire.	
	24th		Wagon Lines were moved to positions in C.20. Bde. Commander and Battery Commanders reconnoitred Battery positions. These were occupied during the afternoon as follows:- "A" Battery J.24.b.4.3. "B" Battery unchanged. "C" Battery J.13.c.1.8. "D" Battery J.19.a.8.9. Enemy Artillery shelled forward areas heavily and persistently, and used some gas shell. Enemy aeroplanes flew over Battery areas at low altitudes during the morning. 15th Brigade R.H.A. attached to this Brigade to assist in Barrage on 25th inst. At night they took up previously reconnoitred positions as follows:- Warwick Bty. J.19.a.9.5., "B" Battery J.19.a.3.4., "L" Battery J.19.c.3.9. 460 Bty. (RFA) J.19.c.1.8.	

Army Form C. 2118.

WAR DIARY
or
INTELLIGENCE SUMMARY.

(Erase heading not required.)

Instructions regarding War Diaries and Intelligence Summaries are contained in F. S. Regs., Part II. and the Staff Manual respectively. Title pages will be prepared in manuscript.

Place	Date	Hour	Summary of Events and Information	Remarks and references to Appendices
	25th		2nd Lieut. J.C.FORSTER, C/153, and 2nd Lt. W.N.SCOTT, D/153, appointed F.O.Os. Barrage opened at 9.0 am supported by 15th Brigade R.H.A. and 113 Brigade R.F.A. Seige and Heavy Artillery were also employed, and Infantry were well satisfied with barrage. At noon "A" and "C" Batteries moved forward in support to J.26.a.7.3. and J.19.c.8.1. respectively. Reports from F.O.Os show that Infantry were held up by M.G. fire from about J.29.a. and that the situation at STERHOEK was obscure. 109th Inf. Bde. H.Q. moved to J.26.a.0.8. at 11.50 am. There was a further barrage at 5.0. pm. and at 21.00 108th Inf. Bde. were reported on the following line — J.23.a.9.0. — J.28.a.5.5. — J.22.d.6.6. — along road in J.22.b. — J.16.c.5.0.— then along railway to 200X S. of HALTE. Position of 109th Inf. Bde. at 22.20 was obscure, and it was doubtful whether they were in touch with the Division on the right. Batteries of 15th Brigade R.H.A. were withdrawn.	
	26th		Front was quiet, and no operations took place. Infantry instructed to dig in on present lines. Warning orders received that Brigade would be relieved by 34th Division, and forward wagon lines instructed to proceed to rear wagon lines in vicinity of SPRIETE. Later when Battery reliefs were complete batteries proceeded to rear wagon lines, and H.Q. to a billet in BEVEREN.	
	27th		Brigade marched to KNOCK, via HARLEBEKE, GUERNE and BISSEGHEM, and were billeted in M.21. (sheet 29) Bde. H.Q. at M.21.a.8.2. All Batteries had arrived at 15.30.	
	28th.		Day was spend overhauling equipment, and adjusting personnel of Batteries.	
	29th.		No change.	
	30th.		M.G.R.A. 2nd Army inspected horses of "A", "B" and "D" Batteries.	
	31st		No change.	

(signature)

Lieut. Col. R.F.A.
Commanding 153rd Brigade R.F.A.

153rd Brigade R.F.A.

Army Form C. 2118.

WAR DIARY
INTELLIGENCE SUMMARY

(Erase heading not required.)

November 1918.

Place	Date	Hour	Summary of Events and Information	Remarks and references to Appendices

LAUWE.	1st.		Brigade Commander and Battery Commanders went forward to reconnoitre positions. Positions were selected as follows:-
			     H.Q. O.35.c.8.5.
			     A/153. U.6.a.10.90.
			     B/153. U.6.a.15.45.
			     C/153. U.6.a.30.75.
			     D/153. U.6.a.00.60.	

	2nd.		Inspection of Brigade in marching order by the Xth Corps Commander.	
	3rd.		Battery Commanders warned to go forward and reconnoitre positions in P.27.a. and P.27.d.	

	4th.		Brigade Commander and Battery Commanders went forward to reconnoitre positions. Positions were selected as follows:-
			     H.Q. P.20.b.5.3.
			     A/153. P.27.a.4.3.
			     B/153. P.27.a.3.5.
			     C/153. P.27.a.30.85.
			     D/153. 2 guns P.27.d.15.10.
			                2 guns P.27.d.0.2.
			                2 guns P.27.d.00.75.	

	5th.		Batteries moved up to Wagon Lines at 11.0 am as follows:- H.Q. N.18.d.4.0. and Batteries in vicinity.	
	6th.		No change.	

	7th.		Brigade Commander and Battery Commanders went forward to reconnoitre new positions. Positions were selected as follows:-
			     H.Q. P.20.a.0.3.
			     A/153. P.26.a.2.8.
			     B/153. P.26.b.2.7.
			     C/153. P.32.a.2.3.
			     D/153. P.32.a.75.75.	

	7th.		Guns moved up to positions selected, with orders to be in position by dawn 8th inst. Ammunition 18-pdr 350 rounds per gun. 4.5" How. 250 rounds per How. Guard only left with guns.	
	8th.		No change.	
	9th.		do	
	10th.		do	

Army Form C. 2118.

WAR DIARY
or
INTELLIGENCE SUMMARY

(Erase heading not required.)

Instructions regarding War Diaries and Intelligence Summaries are contained in F. S. Regs., Part II. and the Staff Manual respectively. Title pages will be prepared in manuscript.

Place	Date	Hour	Summary of Events and Information	Remarks and references to Appendices
	11th		Batteries remained in positions.	
	12th		Batteries received orders to pull out guns and return to wagon lines before dawn. Guns were pulled out, and Batteries marched to TOURCOING area at 10 am. The Brigade arrived at new area at 2.0 pm and were billeted in the town. All the horses under cover.	
	13th		Day devoted to squaring up of equipment.	
	14th		No change.	
	15th		No change.	
	16th		Lt. Col. C.W.M. IVENS proceeded on leave, and Major A.A. MARSON, M.C., took over command of the Brigade.	
	17th		Thanksgiving Service held.	
	18th		Conference re Educational scheme held at MOUSCRON. Corps Commander presided.	
	19th		Educational meeting held, and arrangements made to commence classes at once.	
	20th		Training and general work in progress.	
	21st		do.	
	22nd		31 pairs of horses lent to farmers in neighbourhood of NEUVILLE to assist in agricultural work.	
	23rd		36 pairs of horses lent to farmers. D.A.D.V.S. inspected horses of the Brigade.	
	24th		36 pairs of horses lent to farmers to assist in agricultural work.	
	25th		do.	
	26th		No change.	
	27th		do	
	28th		do	
	29th		Brigade took over convoy work for forage and rations.	
	30th		No change.	

Major R.F.A.
Commanding 153rd Brigade R.F.A.

153rd Brigade R.F.A.

Army Form C. 2118.

WAR DIARY
or
INTELLIGENCE SUMMARY.
(Erase heading not required.)

December 1918.

Place	Date	Hour	Summary of Events and Information	Remarks and references to Appendices
TOURCOING	1st.		No change in location since last month. The Brigade continued to carry out convoy work for supplies for the Divisional Artillery. Education and Sports received attention in weekly programmes.	
	1st to 31st.		ditto.	
	24th		G.O.C., R.A., XVth Corps accompanied by C.R.A. visited the horse lines, billets etc. of all Batteries of the Brigade.	
	25th.		Special Christmas Service held at 11.0 am.	

Lieut. Col. R.F.A.
Commanding 153rd Brigade R.F.A.

36/

WAR DIARY
or
INTELLIGENCE-SUMMARY.
(Erase heading not required.)

153rd Brigade R.F.A.   Army Form C. 2118.

January 1919.

VR 37

Instructions regarding War Diaries and Intelligence Summaries are contained in F. S. Regs., Part II. and the Staff Manual respectively. Title pages will be prepared in manuscript.

Place	Date	Hour	Summary of Events and Information	Remarks and references to Appendices
TOURCOING.	1st to 31st		No change in location. Ordinary routine carried out daily.	

Cluilius
Lieut. Col. R.F.A.
Commanding 153rd Brigade R.F.A.

Army Form C. 2118.

153rd Brigade R.F.A.

Instructions regarding War Diaries and Intelligence Summaries are contained in F. S. Regs., Part II. and the Staff Manual respectively. Title pages will be prepared in manuscript.

WAR DIARY
or
INTELLIGENCE SUMMARY.
(Erase heading not required.)

February 1919.

Vol 38

Place	Date	Hour	Summary of Events and Information	Remarks and references to Appendices
TOURCOING.			No change in location. Ordinary routine carried out daily.	

Signature

Lieut. Col. R.F.A.
Commanding 153rd Brigade R.F.A.

www.ingramcontent.com/pod-product-compliance
Lightning Source LLC
Chambersburg PA
CBHW081529160426
43191CB00011B/1719